Editor-in-Chief
Michael W. Dempsey B.A.

Contributors
Angela Sheehan B.A.
A. T. H. Rowland-Entwhistle F.R.G.S.
Jean Cooke
John Holland B.A.
Francis Halton

Purnell's FIRST ENCYCLOPEDIA

in colour

PURNELL
London

Purnell's FIRST ENCYCLOPEDIA

ACID A lemon tastes sour because there is an acid in it. It is called citric acid. The same acid gives oranges and grapefruit their sharp taste. There are many different acids and they all taste sour. Vinegar is an acid and there is an acid in our stomachs which helps us to digest food.

The acids in our bodies and in the food we eat are all weak and harmless. But some acids are very strong and very dangerous. They burn the skin if they are touched. They can even dissolve metals. Sulphuric acid, nitric acid and hydrochloric acid are three of the strong acids. Strong acids are used to make many things including paints, fertilizers and explosives.

AFRICA Africa is the world's second largest land mass, or continent. It is almost three times the size of Europe. But far fewer people live in Africa than in Europe. In the north of Africa there is a large desert stretching across the continent from coast to coast. It is called the Sahara. Most people in the Sahara live around waterholes and small lakes called oases. There are deserts in southern Africa too though they are not as large as the Sahara.

In the centre of Africa the climate is hot and wet. The land is covered by thick forests where the trees grow so close together that their leaves blot out the sun.

Other parts of Africa are high rolling plains covered with grass and dotted with trees. In the past great herds of animals roamed the grasslands. There were elephants, lions, zebra, giraffes, deer, antelopes and many others. But so many were killed by hunters that some of the animals were in danger of becoming extinct. To save the animals which are left many African countries have set up special parks where the animals can live in peace.

Africa has many great rivers. The longest river in the world, the Nile, flows across the Sahara to the Mediterranean Sea. Millions of people live in the fertile valley of the Nile. The fertile valley of the Nile was the home of one of the first great civilizations—Ancient Egypt. Today millions of people live in the Nile Valley. Other great rivers are the Congo, the Niger and the Zambezi.

Most of the people who live in Africa are Negroes. They belong to many different tribes and speak many different languages. There are also people of European descent who live mainly in the south and Arabs who live mainly in the north.

There is acid in many of the foods we eat

Apple   Pear   Grapes   Rhubarb   Vinegar

Trapping fish on the Congo River

Diamonds are mined
in South Africa

Cairo is Africa's
largest city

Many great dams have been
built across Africa's rivers

Most Africans are farmers. They either rear cattle or grow crops to feed their families. Some crops are grown especially for sale to the rest of the world. These include cotton, tea, cocoa and coffee.

Africa is rich in metals. Copper and uranium are mined in central Africa and much of the world's gold comes from southern Africa. Most diamonds also come from South Africa.

Africa used to be called the dark continent. It got this name because very little was known about it by people of other lands. Africa was very difficult to explore. Swamps, dense forests and deserts made it difficult

to travel on foot. Huge waterfalls and rapids made it impossible to travel far by boat. Despite these difficulties, Europeans slowly explored the continent and claimed the lands they discovered for their own countries. Africa soon became a continent of colonies ruled by European countries. Today most of the colonies have gained their independence.

AIR The air we breathe is a mixture of gases. Over three-quarters of it is nitrogen. Less than one quarter is oxygen, the gas all animals need to live. There are small amounts of other gases, too. The most important is carbon dioxide. This is the gas plants need in order to make their food.

Air surrounds the Earth to a height of several hundred miles. This covering of air is called the atmosphere. During the day the atmosphere protects the Earth from much of the Sun's heat. During the night it acts like a blanket, holding the heat in. Without the atmosphere it would be far too hot during the day and far too cold at night for plants or animals to live on Earth.

The air around the Earth weighs many millions of tons. The column of air above each person's head weighs about one ton. We do not feel this great weight because the pressure is equal all over our bodies, both inside and outside.

AIRCRAFT Men first tried to fly by imitating birds. They strapped artificial wings to their arms and flapped them. But their muscles were not strong enough to lift them from the ground. At last people gave up copying birds and began to design machines with wings that did not move. At first they built gliders and launched them from the tops of hills. The gliders sank to the ground unless rising air currents kept them aloft for a while. Then, in 1903, the first real aeroplane flew. The American brothers, Wilbur and Orville Wright made short flights in a machine made of wood, cloth and wire, and powered by a petrol engine turning a propeller. From then on aeroplanes were rapidly improved. Today giant airliners carrying hundreds of people fly several miles above the Earth to every part of the world.

The lift which keeps an aeroplane weighing hundreds of tons in the air comes from the shape of its wings. These are curved on the top and flat underneath. As the aeroplane moves forward the air flows past its wings. Air flowing over the curved top of the wing has farther to go than air flowing underneath the wing. This difference creates a suction which lifts the aeroplane upwards.

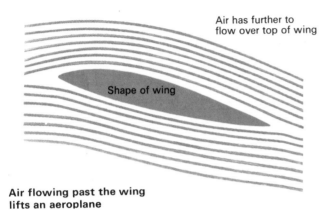

Air has further to flow over top of wing

Shape of wing

Air flowing past the wing lifts an aeroplane

To stay in the air an aeroplane must keep moving forwards. Some aeroplanes are driven by propellers turned by piston engines. The blades of a propeller are shaped rather like aeroplane wings. As the propeller turns it produces a thrust which pulls the aeroplane forwards rather like a screw going through wood.

A jet engine

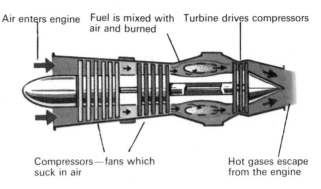

Air enters engine   Fuel is mixed with air and burned   Turbine drives compressors

Compressors—fans which suck in air   Hot gases escape from the engine

Most modern aeroplanes are powered by jet engines. Jet engines do not need propellers and they are more powerful than piston engines. In a jet engine air is sucked in by a special kind of fan. Then it is mixed with fuel and burned. This produces hot gases which escape out of the back of the engine. The rush of these gases backwards drives the aeroplane forwards.

On the wings and tail of an aeroplane are movable parts. The pilot uses these to make the aeroplane go up or down or to turn. The cockpit of a modern aeroplane contains many instruments. Some tell the pilot how the various systems of the aeroplane are working. Others tell him his height, his speed through the air, and the direction in which the aeroplane is heading.

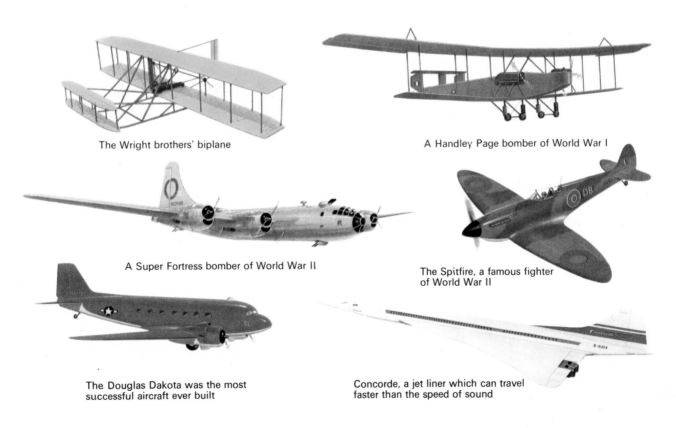

The Wright brothers' biplane

A Handley Page bomber of World War I

A Super Fortress bomber of World War II

The Spitfire, a famous fighter of World War II

The Douglas Dakota was the most successful aircraft ever built

Concorde, a jet liner which can travel faster than the speed of sound

AIRPORT Aeroplanes begin and end their flights at airports. There are so many airliners flying to all parts of the world that at big airports they take off and land every minute or so.

The most important people at an airport are the air-traffic controllers in the control tower. As an airliner approaches an airport the pilot calls up the control tower by radio. If the runways are full the controller tells the pilot to join the queue of airliners waiting to land. The airliners fly in circles one above the other. When the bottom airliner is given permission to land the rest move down one level. This is called stacking.

The controller can see the airliners in the sky on his radar screen. He uses radio to guide them down safely to the runway. When an airliner lands it is travelling so fast that it needs a long distance in which to stop. Some runways are several miles long.

As soon as an airliner has landed it moves along a taxiway to an area called an apron.

Trucks to carry baggage and buses to carry passengers hurry towards it. Then tankers move in to refuel the airliner's fuel tanks. Soon the airliner is ready for its next flight.

ALPHABET An alphabet is a group of letters used to write down a language. English is written in the Roman alphabet which has 26 letters. Most other European languages are written in this alphabet but the letters are sometimes pronounced in different ways. The Greek alphabet has 24 letters. It is used only in Greece although scientists use the letters as signs in their work. The word alphabet comes from the first two letters of the Greek alphabet. A is called alpha and B is called beta. One of the smallest alphabets is used in the Hawaiian language. It has only 12 letters.

AMPHIBIANS The name amphibian means double life. Amphibians are animals which spend part of their life on land and part in

Air-traffic controllers in the control tower guide planes in to land and tell the pilots when they can take off. Radar screens show where the planes are in the sky and on the ground

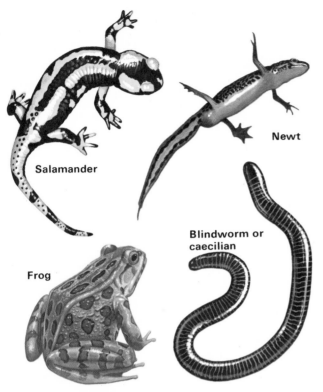

Salamander

Newt

Frog

Blindworm or caecilian

few amphibians never grow up. They keep their gills for the rest of their lives.

Amphibians also breathe through their skins which must be kept moist. This is why amphibians live in damp places and hide from the sunlight.

ANTS Ants are called social insects because they live and work in groups called colonies. There may be many thousands of ants in a colony each with its own special duty. Most colonies live in nests either on the ground or in trees. Ant hills on the ground contain many rooms joined by tunnels in which the ants store food and look after their young.

A colony consists of a queen ant, male ants and worker ants. Worker ants are small female ants that do not lay eggs. The workers repair the nest, collect the food and look after the young. Sometimes there are large worker ants with powerful jaws to defend the nest from other ants. These are called soldiers.

fresh water. They include frogs and toads, newts and salamanders and strange worm-like animals called caecilians or blind-worms. Newts spend most of their time in water. Frogs and toads are at home both on land and in water. Salamanders spend most of their time on land. But nearly all amphibians must return to water to breed because their eggs do not have shells and would dry up on land.

When the eggs hatch the young amphibians breathe through gills like fish. As they grow up and leave the water they breathe through lungs like other land animals. A

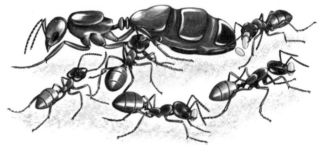

Worker ants carry away the eggs laid by the queen and look after the young which hatch from them

APES Of all animals, apes are the most similar to man. They have similar bodies, except that their arms are longer and their legs are shorter. They are the only other animals to walk upright. And they are more intelligent than any other creature except man.

Chimpanzees are very intelligent and very playful. They can be taught to do many things like painting or drinking tea from a cup

Apes live in family groups in forests eating fruit and other plant food. They include gorillas, chimpanzees, orang-utans and gibbons. Gorillas and chimpanzees live in Africa. The others live in Asia.

Gorillas are the largest of the apes. They are as tall as a man and extremely strong. Chimpanzees are very intelligent and very curious. Both gorillas and chimpanzees live mainly on the ground, but they sleep in the trees. Orang-utans are the only apes to live entirely in the trees. Their name means 'man of the woods' and they do look very human. Gibbons have very long arms which reach to the ground when they stand up. Their long arms help gibbons to swing swiftly from branch to branch through the forest.

An Aquarium

AQUARIUM An aquarium is a tank for keeping fishes and other water animals. It usually has glass sides so that the animals can be seen easily. A simple aquarium can be made from a glass tank or bowl. The bottom should be covered with sand and gravel. Then clean water can be gently poured in.

Water plants make an aquarium look attractive. They also provide the fishes with oxygen. Pond snails help to keep an aquarium clean. They eat tiny green plants called algae which grow in the water and on the glass. The aquarium should be kept in a bright place, but not in sunlight.

An aquarium can only support a certain number of fish. If there are too many fish, some will rise to the surface of the water and gasp. Aquarium fish can be fed with special food bought from pet shops. They should be given only as much food as they can eat in ten minutes.

ARCHAEOLOGY The word archaeology comes from two Greek words. One means old. The other means study. Archaeology means learning about people of long ago. The clues are the belongings the people left behind them—bones, tools, ornaments, pottery, coins and buildings. Often the clues are buried under the ground. They are found when archaeologists dig up the site of an old building or a vanished city. From the clues that are found archaeologists try to build up a picture of the lives of the people who lived there—what they ate, how they made their living, what tools they used, and what skills they had developed.

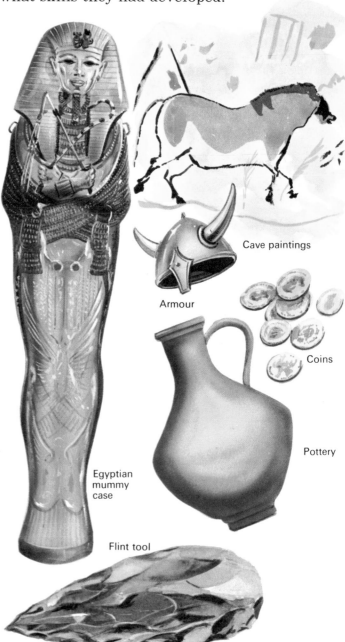

Cave paintings

Armour

Coins

Egyptian mummy case

Pottery

Flint tool

We learn about people of long ago from the paintings and belongings they left behind them

Greek temple

Chinese temple

Castle

Skyscraper

Egyptian pyramid

Roman stadium

Gothic cathedral

Not all archaeology is done by excavating. By looking at photographs taken from the air archaeologists may discover the outline of a vanished building or town. Crops grow shorter over stones than over deep soil and this difference shows up clearly from the air. Much has also been learned about ancient peoples from ancient manuscripts and writings on stone tablets. Sometimes it has taken years for archaeologists to work out what these writings mean.

ARCHITECTURE Architecture is the art of designing buildings.

The first great architects were the Ancient Egyptians. They built huge temples and tombs which have lasted for thousands of years. They built smaller buildings from baked clay and reeds.

The Ancient Greeks were also fine architects. They made their buildings from columns supporting beams on which the roof rested. The Greeks tried to be perfect in everything they did. Their buildings are among the finest and most beautiful ever made.

The Ancient Romans copied Greek ideas. They also invented the arch and the vault. A vault is a roof which is supported by arches. The Romans were able to make taller buildings in this way. They also used arches to build great bridges.

Many different materials have been used by architects to make their buildings. For thousands of years buildings were made of wood, stone, or bricks of baked clay. Only stone was strong enough to make very big buildings, and these took years to build. Today, big buildings are made from steel and concrete.

ARMOUR Special clothing that protects a person against weapons is called armour. The first armour was made of leather. Then men made metal shields, helmets and breastplates. Armour grew heavier and heavier.

When knights rode into battle on horses, they were covered from head to toe in armour. It was so heavy that the knights could not climb on their horses. They were lifted into the saddle by a crane.

As soon as guns were invented, armour was useless. It could not protect soldiers against bullets. For a long time afterwards, the only armour soldiers wore was a steel helmet. Now new bullet-proof materials have been invented which are light enough to be worn. Some soldiers wear bullet-proof waistcoats made of tough plastic or metal.

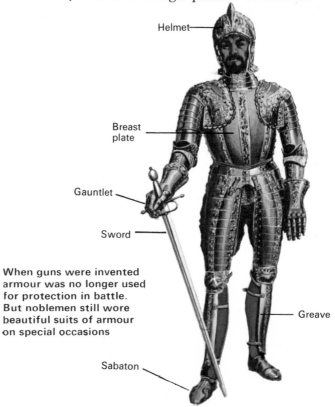

Helmet

Breast plate

Gauntlet

Sword

Greave

When guns were invented armour was no longer used for protection in battle. But noblemen still wore beautiful suits of armour on special occasions

Sabaton

13

Asia has many crowded cities

Buffaloes pull ploughs in the rice fields of Asia. Few farmers can afford to buy tractors

Japan has many modern factories

ASIA More than half of all the people in the world live in Asia. Asia is the largest of the continents.

Asia has the highest mountains in the world. They are called the Himalaya. The highest peak in the Himalaya is Mount Everest. Near the Himalaya are the high, wind-swept plains of Tibet. They are sometimes called the roof of the world because they are so high and flat.

In the north of Asia is the largest amount of flat land in the world. This is the great Siberian plain which stretches for thousands of miles across the continent. Few people live in Siberia. Most of it is covered by forests of firs and pines where tigers and wolves roam.

Asia has many deserts. They are not the largest deserts in the world but they are among the driest. The biggest desert is the Gobi. There are few waterholes in the Gobi Desert. Other parts of Asia have more rain than anywhere else in the world. But most of the rain falls during a few months of summer when wet winds blow in from the sea. It sometimes rains for weeks on end without a break.

Most of Asia's people live in the fertile river valleys of India and China. There are so many people that farmland is very scarce. Many farmers find it difficult to provide enough food for their families from their small farms. The most important crop in India and China is rice. Some families have little else to eat. Modern ways of farming are being taught and tractors are slowly taking the place of buffaloes for pulling ploughs, but it will be a long time before people in the crowded parts of Asia have enough to eat.

In many parts of Asia all of the things which people need to buy are made in their own villages, from shoes and clothes to pots and pans. Now many new factories have been built. Japan has many factories. The factories of Japan make ships, television sets, cameras and clothes for sale to the rest of the world.

ASTRONAUT The men and women who travel in space are called astronauts. Astronauts must train for a long time before they can be launched into space. They must know how every piece of spacecraft equipment works and what to do in an emergency. They must also be very fit to withstand the tremendous forces of launching and landing.

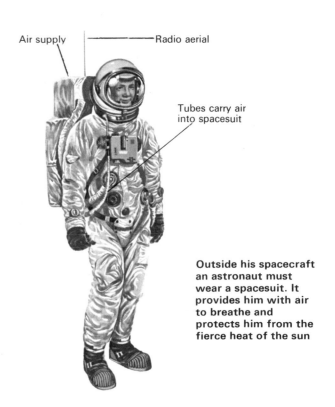

Air supply — Radio aerial

Tubes carry air into spacesuit

Outside his spacecraft an astronaut must wear a spacesuit. It provides him with air to breathe and protects him from the fierce heat of the sun

Electrons whirl around the middle of an atom like the planets circle the Sun

Up in space the astronauts, like everything else, are weightless. At first they find this peculiar. But they soon get used to floating around the spacecraft.

There is no air in space. Nor is there air on the Moon. Whenever the astronauts leave their spacecraft they must wear a spacesuit. This provides them with air to breathe. It also protects them from the fierce heat of the Sun during the day and the bitter cold at night.

ATOM Everything in the world is made of very, very small specks called atoms. Atoms are far too small to be seen even with the most powerful microscope. They are so small that many millions would fit on a pin head.

Scientists once thought that atoms were tiny, solid balls. Now they know that atoms are made of even tinier specks of matter called protons, neutrons and electrons. The electrons whirl around a cluster of protons and neutrons like the planets circle the Sun. Most of an atom is empty space.

AUSTRALIA Australia is the world's largest island. It is almost as big as the whole of Europe. But it has far fewer people than Europe.

Australia is a dry land. Much of it is desert. In other parts it is too dry to grow crops but there is enough grass to feed animals. More sheep are kept in Australia than in any other country. There are far more sheep than people in Australia. The sheep are bred mainly for their wool which is sold to the rest of the world. The sheep are kept on farms called stations. The people living on the stations may be a hundred miles from their nearest neighbour.

Although much of Australia is dry there is plenty of good farmland. Australian farmers grow a lot of wheat. There are so few people in Australia that they sell most of the wheat to other countries.

Australia is rich in metals. There is a lot of iron, gold and silver as well as many other metals.

Many strange animals live in Australia. They include animals with a pouch in which the mother rears her young. These animals are called marsupials. The largest marsupials are kangaroos.

The first people to live in Australia were the dark-skinned Aborigines. Then people began to arrive from Europe. For a long time most Australians worked on farms. They had to buy goods made in factories from other countries. Now Australia has many factories of its own.

The 'flying doctor' visits remote sheep stations

Aborigine with boomerang

Rabbits have destroyed a lot of grassland

Sheep shearing

Sydney Harbour Bridge

AUTOMOBILE The automobile or motor-car is one of the most useful things we have. With a car we can travel from one place to another without having to change our way of travelling. Every year, more than 20 million cars are made in the world—enough to give one to every man, woman, and child in Canada or Yugoslavia. And each car may have as many as 15,000 parts in it!

A motor-car is driven by a machine called an internal combustion engine. It gets its name because the fuel that drives it is com-busted, or burned, right inside the engine. In an old-fashioned kind of engine such as a steam-engine the fuel was burned in a kind of fireplace. It heated a tank of water, which turned into steam. The steam drove the engine.

A car engine is driven by burning petrol, or gasoline. Inside the engine are several cylinders, or tubes, inside which a piston moves up and down—just like a bicycle pump. The piston is attached to a rod, called a crank, which drives a wheel, like the pedals drive the chain of your bicycle. Car engines have four, six, or eight cylinders. Most engines work on what is called the *four-stroke* system. In this system, each piston makes four strokes, two up and two down, but only one of these strokes provides power—just as though you only pressed every other down stroke on your bicycle pedals.

The petrol is mixed with air to make it burn. It is sprayed into the top of each cylinder by the carburettor, which works a bit like a scent-spray. As the fuel and air come in, the piston moves down to draw them in more quickly. Then the piston moves up again to compress the mixture of air and petrol. On the third stroke, an electric stroke sets the fuel alight. It burns very quickly indeed, and expands as it

burns. As it expands, it forces the piston down. This is the power stroke. Finally, the piston moves up again to clear all the gas and smoke out of the cylinder ready for some more fuel. Because there are four or more cylinders, there is always one piston receiving power to drive the car. During the four strokes valves open and close to let the fuel in and the gases out.

The pistons drive a crankshaft, which leads to the gearbox. The gearbox alters the power of the engine, just as your bicycle gearbox does. To go up hill, the driver engages a low gear. The engine moves round very quickly while the car moves slowly and powerfully. The car can climb steep hills in low gear. In high gear, the engine runs more slowly because it has less work to do, and the car runs smoothly along a level road. The clutch is a device which enables the driver to interrupt the drive from the engine so that he can change gear. More driving shafts and gears take the driving force from the gearbox to the wheels to move the car along.

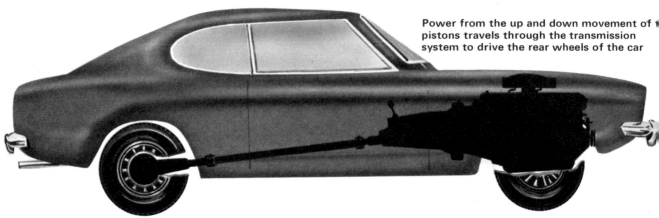

Power from the up and down movement of the pistons travels through the transmission system to drive the rear wheels of the car

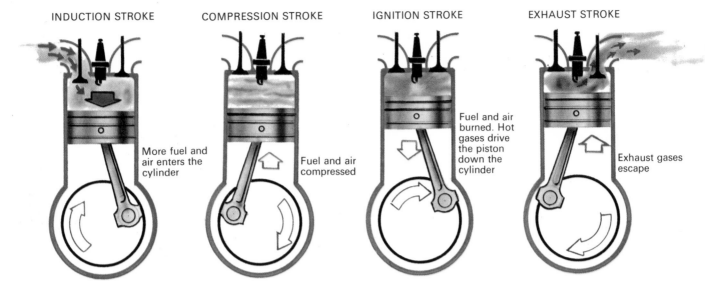

How a four stroke engine works

INDUCTION STROKE

More fuel and air enters the cylinder

COMPRESSION STROKE

Fuel and air compressed

IGNITION STROKE

Fuel and air burned. Hot gases drive the piston down the cylinder

EXHAUST STROKE

Exhaust gases escape

A car engine will not start itself. It has to be spun, and then it will spring into life. An electric starter-motor, driven by the car's battery, turns the engine to make it start. The battery also supplies the sparks to make the fuel burn. When the car is running, a dynamo puts more electricity into the battery.

BACTERIA The tiniest living things in the world—millions upon millions of them— are everywhere around us. They are so small that a thousand of them would be only as big as a dot made with a sharp pencil. We call them *bacteria*. Some of them are harmful to us and cause diseases. People often refer to them as *germs*. Others are very useful indeed. Some help to make the soil rich, so that plants can feed on it. Others cause changes in food. Without them we could not make wine, or vinegar, or cheese. But they can also turn food bad, which is why we freeze it or seal it up in cans or packets so that the bacteria cannot operate.

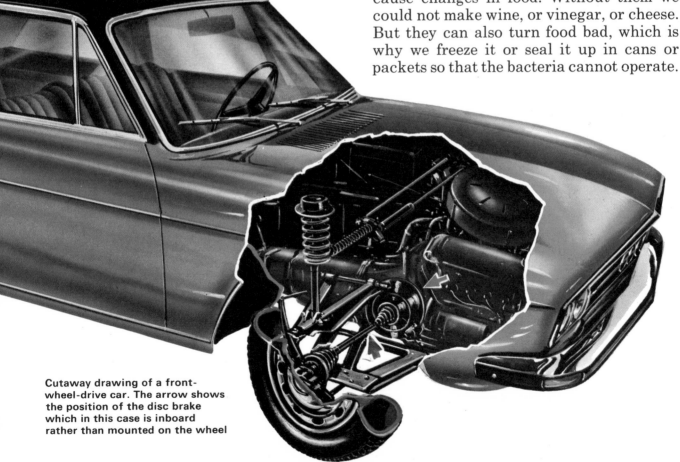

Cutaway drawing of a front-wheel-drive car. The arrow shows the position of the disc brake which in this case is inboard rather than mounted on the wheel

17

The shy badger lives in the woods

BADGER The badger is a meat-eating animal with a heavy body, short legs and a long snout. It has shaggy grey or brownish fur with black and white stripes on the head and neck.

Badgers live in deep burrows called sets. They sleep by day and come out at night to hunt for food. They eat mainly small animals such as rats, mice and young rabbits.

Badgers have very sharp claws and will fight fiercely if they are trapped by an enemy.

The five main positions of the feet in ballet

BALLET Ballet is a special dance set to music. It may tell a story or it may bring out the meaning of the music through the movement of the dancers.

Several people help to make a ballet. The composer writes the music. The choreographer works out the steps of the dancers. The designer creates ideas for the scenery, costumes and lighting. The dancers and the orchestra must rehearse many times before the ballet is performed.

Rules for the correct steps in ballet were made hundreds of years ago in France. They are based mainly on five positions of the feet. These positions are planned to make the body balanced in any position.

BALLOONS Long before aeroplanes were invented, men flew in balloons. The very first balloon flight was made almost two hundred years ago in France. The balloon was a huge cloth bag filled with hot air. The passengers sat in a basket underneath. When the balloon was released it rose high in the air because hot air always rises.

Airships were far bigger than the largest airliners which fly today

You can make a simple hot-air balloon by holding a paper bag upside down over a hot radiator. The bag will fill with hot air and if you let it go it will float until the air cools. Hot air balloons carried a fire in a basket slung underneath to keep the air hot.

Another kind of balloon was filled with a gas which is lighter than air. Stones were carried in the basket under the balloon. They could be thrown over the side to make the balloon rise higher. Gas could be let out of the balloon to make it land.

Airships were invented much later. An airship is a gas-filled balloon with a propeller driven by an engine. Balloons can go only where the wind blows them. Airships can go where the passengers want. The biggest airships were built in Germany. They were much bigger than any aeroplane ever built. They carried many passengers across the Atlantic Ocean. Airships used a gas that caught fire very easily. After a lot of accidents, people stopped building them. Airships were replaced by aeroplanes.

Today, ballooning is a popular sport. Balloons are also used in weather forecasting. They carry instruments which measure the weather high in the sky and send the information by radio back to the ground.

BANKS Banks take care of people's money and use it to make more money. They do this by lending some of the money they are keeping to people who want to borrow money. The banks charge the people who borrow money a fee. This fee is called interest.

There are different kinds of banks. Commercial banks are the ones you see in every town. People put their wages in these banks and the banks help them by taking care of their money, by making it easy for them to pay bills, and by giving them advice.

Bats are the only mammals which can fly. Their wings are made of skin

BATS Bats are the only mammals that fly. They have small furry bodies rather like those of mice, and broad, thin wings made of skin.

Some bats eat fruit. Some eat insects. Some feed on the blood of other animals. These are called vampires.

Most bats have poor eyesight. Yet they fly in the dark without ever bumping in to anything. Bats do not use their eyes for finding their way around. Instead, they send out high-pitched squeaks. Then they listen for the echo. If the echo comes back quickly, they know there is something in the way.

BEAR In many stories bears are shown as friendly animals. But they are really very dangerous. In the wild, a bear will attack and kill a person with no warning. Bears normally eat small animals of all kinds. They also eat plant food and are fond of honey.

Bears are close relatives of dogs, but they are much larger and have no tail. Their body is covered with shaggy fur and they have powerful legs with strong claws.

Polar bears are among the biggest bears. They live in the cold Arctic where their whitish fur makes them almost invisible against the snow.

Almost as big is the grizzly bear of North America. This is the most dangerous bear.

Biggest of all is the grizzly bear of North America. It is very popular in the big National Parks.

Bear

BEAVER Many animals build homes to live in. But no animal can match the beaver. This little animal builds big dams across rivers. Beavers fell trees near the river bank using their sharp front teeth to gnaw through the wood. Then they dig a ditch and float the trees down to the dam.

By damming a river the beavers make a pond. In the middle of the pond they build a large home called a lodge. The entrances to the lodge are underwater so that no other animals can get inside.

Beavers have webbed feet which help them swim quickly through the water. They also have a broad, flat tail which they use as an oar and a rudder. Beavers slap their tails on the water to warn of danger.

BEES Bees are very useful insects. Honey bees make the honey we eat. Much more important is the way bees carry pollen from flower to flower. Plants cannot make seeds

Some cells in the honeycomb are used to store honey. Eggs are laid in other cells

unless they are pollinated.

Honey bees and bumble bees are social insects. They live and work together in a home called a hive. There are three kinds of bees in a hive. There are workers, drones and a queen.

The queen bee does nothing but lay eggs. Worker bees hatch from most of the eggs. These are small female bees which do not lay eggs. The workers look after the whole hive. They build the honeycomb in which honey is made and eggs are stored. They collect nectar and pollen from flowers. And they feed the young bees. They also guard the hive, but they sting human beings only if they are frightened. Drones are male bees which do no work and have no sting.

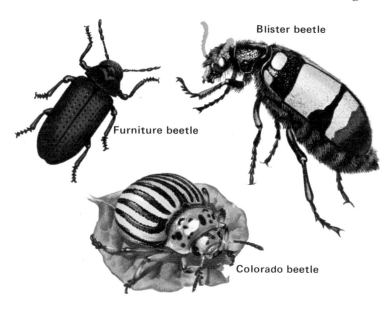

Blister beetle

Furniture beetle

Colorado beetle

BEETLES There are many different kinds of beetles. They are one of the largest groups of insects. Most beetles are small. The largest lives in Africa. It is as big as the palm of your hand.

All beetles have a pair of hard wings. Most beetles have a second pair of thin wings which are used for flying. These are stored under the hard wings when the insect is not in flight.

Many beetles live in the water. Diving beetles spend a long time under water. They trap a bubble of air under their hard wings and carry it down with them. In this way they can breathe under water.

Some beetles are pests. The Colorado beetle damages potato crops. The furniture beetle or woodworm attacks our homes. And grain weevils destroy grain and flour.

BIBLE The Bible is the holy book of the Christian Church. It contains two parts—the Old Testament and the New Testament.

The Old Testament is made up of 39 books. It contains most of the Jewish scriptures. The Old Testament was first written in Hebrew. The New Testament contains 27 books. It describes the life and teachings of Jesus Christ. The New Testament was first written in Greek.

There have been different translations of the Bible into the English language. It has also been translated into over one thousand other languages. More copies of the Bible are sold each year than of any other book.

BIRDS It is impossible to mistake a bird for any other animal. All birds have wings, although some cannot fly. They all have feathers. And they all have a beak.

Scientists believe that birds have descended from reptiles. Birds still have scales on their legs like reptiles. And they lay eggs with a hard shell. The first birds probably glided from tree to tree. As time went on birds flew better and better. The body of a modern bird is wonderfully built for flight. Its bones are hollow and light and its wing muscles are very powerful. A bird's wings are really its front legs. They have long strong feathers needed for flight.

Birds use up a lot of energy and they have to spend a great deal of time eating. A bird's beak takes the place of teeth in other animals. The beak can tear, cut or crack food, but it cannot chew. Different birds have different shaped beaks. Seed-eating birds have short, strong beaks which can

Some birds' eggs: 1 Turkey vulture, 2 Golden eagle,
3 Cassowary, 4 Slaty-backed gull, 5 Spruce grouse,
6 Inca tern, 7 American jacana, 8 American robin,
9 Broad-billed hummingbird, 10 Bird of paradise,
11 Common crow

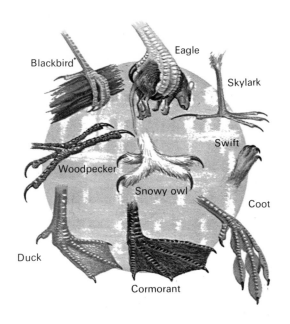

The feet of birds are well suited to the kind of life they lead

Birds are the only animals that have feathers. The centre of a feather is a strong shaft. Where it joins the body the shaft is bare and is called a quill. The flat part of a feather is called the vane. It is made of separate barbs kept together by hooked barbules

The bullfinch has a strong seed-cracking beak

The eagle has a sharp flesh-tearing beak

crack hard seeds. Woodpeckers use their long strong beaks for digging insects out of trees. Ducks have broad, flat beaks for sifting small creatures from the mud and water. And birds of prey have sharp hooked beaks for tearing flesh.

The feet of birds differ too. Swimming birds have webbed feet which they use as paddles. Perching birds have three toes pointing forwards and one toe pointing backwards. This helps them hold on to a branch firmly. Woodpeckers have two toes pointing forwards and two toes pointing backwards. This helps them climb trees without slipping. Birds of prey have sharp talons to grasp their prey.

All birds reproduce by laying eggs. Egg-laying time is called the breeding season. The birds start by choosing their mates. Male birds often have bright colours and special songs to attract a mate.

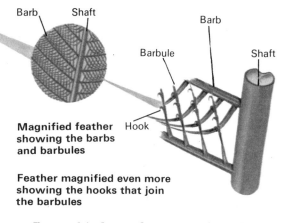

Magnified feather showing the barbs and barbules

Feather magnified even more showing the hooks that join the barbules

Some birds make nests in which to lay their eggs. Others use a hollow in the ground. Most nests are made of grass, mud and twigs, but some birds build strange nests. Tailor birds make their nest from two leaves sewn together. The weaver bird was given its name because it weaves a hanging bottle-shaped nest from grass.

Most birds lay about half a dozen eggs. After being laid, the eggs have to be kept warm. The birds do this by sitting on their eggs. Sometimes only one parent will sit on the eggs. Sometimes both parents take it in turns. The sitting bird is fed by its partner. The eggs hatch in two to three weeks. Then the parents spend all their time feeding their young. Nestling birds grow very quickly and after a few weeks they are ready for their first flying lesson.

BRAILLE Braille is a special way of writing that blind people can understand. Raised dots are printed on the page instead of the letters of the alphabet. Different patterns of dots mean different letters or words. Blind people can touch the dots and understand the words. Some of them learn to read braille very fast.

Blind people can also write braille on a braillewriter. This is a machine like a typewriter which stamps out the dots.

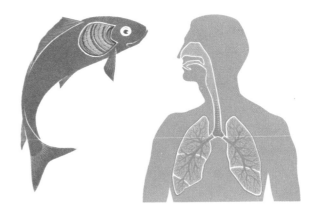

Louis Braille's alphabet and
five short forms of words

BRAIN The brain is rather like the control tower of an airport. Everything that happens at an airport is controlled from the tower. Everything that you do is controlled by your brain. Every animal has a brain, but none has a brain as big for the size of its body as man's.

The brain receives messages from our senses. When you want to pick up a pencil, your brain sends a message to the muscles in your arm so that you are able to stretch and pick it up.

Different parts of the brain control different things. One part enables us to speak to each other. Other parts control hearing, seeing, feeling and so on. The brain is also the place where thinking takes place and where we 'store' everything we know.

BREATHING All animals and plants need a gas from the air called oxygen. We get the oxygen we need when we breathe. We breathe in oxygen and breathe out a gas called carbon dioxide. People breathe with lungs. The lungs are like two spongy bags. Air is taken into them through the windpipe, a tube that runs from the nose to the lungs. The oxygen in the air goes through the walls of the lungs into the blood. The blood carries the oxygen to every tiny part, or cell, of the body.

Fishes breathe through gills. They take in water through their mouths and force it

Fish breathe with gills. People breathe with lungs

out of their bodies over the gills. Oxygen dissolved in the water passes through the gill walls into the fish's blood as the water goes out.

Insects do not have lungs or gills. They have tiny holes on the outside of their body. The air goes through the holes into tiny breathing tubes which carry oxygen to all parts of the body. Some animals can 'breathe' through their skins. The oxygen in the air or water goes straight into their blood.

BRIDGE The first bridge made by man was probably a tree trunk laid across a stream. Bridges like this are still built today, but now they are made of steel and concrete. They are called beam bridges. When beam bridges are built across wide rivers they must be supported by piers to prevent them collapsing.

The ancient Romans invented the arch and used it to build strong stone bridges. Some of their bridges are standing today. The famous Sydney Harbour Bridge is made of a great steel arch.

The biggest bridges of all are suspension bridges. The roadway hangs from strong wire cables which are slung over tall towers and anchored firmly in the ground. One of the most famous suspension bridges is the Golden Gate Bridge which spans the entrance to San Fransisco harbour in America.

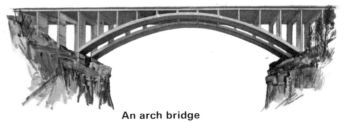

An arch bridge

BULBS All plants make food for themselves when their leaves are green but they do not use it all at once. They store some of it to use later. Some plants, like daffodils and tulips, store their extra food in special leaves, called bulbs. The best known bulb is the onion. If you cut an onion in half you will see the layers of fleshy leaves around a tiny bud. The plant stores the food in the bulb during the winter. In spring it uses the food to make new leaves and shoots.

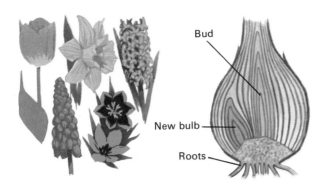

Many flowers grow from bulbs. A bulb is made of fleshy leaves

BUTTER We eat butter on bread and use it for frying and making cakes. It is made from the rich fat in the cream of milk. The fat is separated from the rest of the cream by 'churning', or beating. Years ago farmers used to churn butter by hand in big wooden tubs. Now butter is made by machines in factories.

BUTTERFLIES AND MOTHS The most beautiful insects are the butterflies. They have big wings with lovely colours and patterns. The colours come from tiny scales all over them. Moths fly mostly at night. Many of them are small and dull but not all of them. Some of the moths that live in hotter countries are bright greens and reds and their wings are as wide as this page.

Butterflies and moths are born from eggs. Each egg hatches into a larva, called a caterpillar. The caterpillar eats until it becomes so big that its skin splits and falls off. Underneath a new, bigger skin has already grown so the caterpillar can go on eating until it is ready for a new skin again. The caterpillar 'moults' like this several times until it is fully grown. Then it stops eating and attaches itself to a leaf or twig. The outside of its body hardens into a stiff case, called a chrysalis. Inside the case, the caterpillar's body slowly changes its shape. After some time the case splits and out comes a beautiful butterfly. It waits for its wings to dry and then flies away to feed on the flowers.

Some moth caterpillars spin cocoons of silk in which to rest while they turn into adults. Some spin the very strong silk that is used to make dress material. But not all moths are as useful as the silkworm moths. The clothes moth lays its eggs in clothes hanging in the wardrobe. When the eggs hatch the tiny caterpillars eat holes in the cloth. Other caterpillars feed on leaves and other parts of plants. They do a lot of damage to crops. But butterflies and moths help the flowers as well. They carry pollen from flower to flower as they search for nectar. This helps the plants to produce new seeds and flowers.

The caterpillar of the clothes moth eats holes in cloth

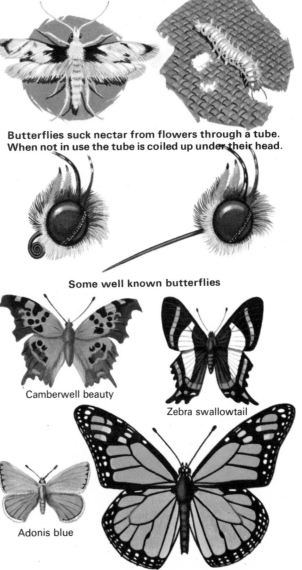

Butterflies suck nectar from flowers through a tube. When not in use the tube is coiled up under their head.

Some well known butterflies

Camberwell beauty

Zebra swallowtail

Adonis blue

Monarch or milkweed

23

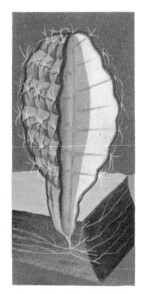

Cacti have no leaves. Instead they are covered with spines

Cacti store water in their swollen stems

CAMEL The camel is often called the ship of the desert. Camels have been used for many years to carry people and their goods on long journeys across the deserts of Asia and Africa.

The camel is well suited to desert travel. It can go longer than most animals without food or water. It stores food in its hump and it has wide, padded feet which stop it sinking into the sand.

Bactrian camel   Arabian camel

CACTUS Cacti are flowering plants which live in the deserts of America. Most cacti have wide-spreading roots to soak up as much moisture as possible when it rains. They also have fat, fleshy stems in which the water can be stored.

Because they contain water, cacti would be good food for the animals living in the desert. Most cacti are covered with prickles which keep them from being eaten.

There are two kinds of camels. The bactrian camel of central Asia has two humps. The Arabian camel has one hump. A dromedary is a kind of Arabian camel which can run very fast.

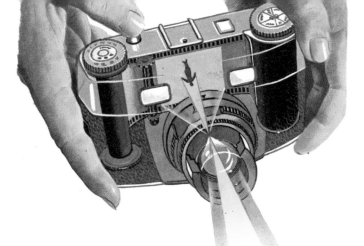

The lens of a camera throws a picture of what is in front of it on to a film at the back

CAMERA A camera is used to take photographs. It is simply a light-tight box. Light can only enter a camera when a shutter is pulled away from a small opening in the front. When this happens, the light shines through a glass lens. The lens throws a picture of what is in front of it onto a strip of material at the back of the camera called a film. The film is coated with a chemical which is sensitive to light. The picture on the film is invisible until the film has been treated with chemicals. This is called developing.

CANAL A canal is a man-made river. Long ago most heavy goods were carried in barges along canals. The barges were towed by horses walking along a tow-path.

Canals were not easy to build. Sometimes they had to cross hills. This was done by building locks in the canals. A lock is a chamber with watertight doors at either end. Water can be let into a lock or let out of it to raise or lower barges from one level to another.

When roads and railways were built, canals were used less and less for moving heavy goods. Today, the most important canals are those which link the oceans. The Panama Canal allows ships to sail from the Atlantic to the Pacific Ocean without going around South America. The Suez Canal links the Mediterranean Sea with the Indian Ocean.

A lock has watertight gates at either end. Water can be let into the lock and let out of it to raise or lower boats from one level of the canal to another

CASTLES In the days when there were no strong nations, each nobleman had to protect his own family and all the people who lived on his lands. So the noblemen built castles in which everyone could shelter when they were attacked.

The first castles were made of wood. Later they were built of stone. Castles were often built on hills. This made them difficult to attack. Castles built on level ground had a moat around them for extra protection. A drawbridge let people cross the moat. It could be raised when the castle was attacked.

The outer walls of a castle were tall and strong. There were towers along the walls. The towers had windows from which archers could fire their arrows.

Battering rams, scaling ladders, arrows and huge stones hurled by machines called catapults were used to attack castles before the invention of gunpowder. Often the siege went on for a long time and sometimes the defenders were forced to surrender through lack of food and water

Inside the walls were stables and store-houses. There was also enough room to graze a few animals. There had to be sufficient food to feed the people for a long time. In the middle of the castle was a big tower called a keep. This was the safest part of the castle. The nobleman's family and servants lived in the keep.

Castles were not comfortable places to live in. They were dark, cold and draughty. There was very little furniture. And the rooms were always filled with smoke from the fires and the torches on the walls.

When guns were invented, people stopped building castles. The walls of a castle could easily be smashed by cannon-balls.

Cats have sharp teeth and claws

CATS Lions, tigers, cheetahs and domestic cats all belong to the cat family. Cats are meat-eating animals and hunt for their food. The only animals a domestic cat is likely to catch are mice and birds. But it hunts them in the same way that a lion or tiger hunts its prey. Cats creep quietly towards their prey on soft, padded feet. Then they leap and kill the animal with one blow of their paw or with their sharp claws.

All cats have very sharp teeth. They all have long, sensitive whiskers on their head. And most have claws which can be drawn in to protect the sharp points.

Shorthorn cow   Highland cow

CATTLE Beef, milk, butter and cheese all come from cattle. They are the most important farm animals. Some cattle are kept for their meat. Others are kept for their milk.

Cattle belong to the ox family, together with buffalo and bison. They are large unintelligent animals. Most cattle have horns, but there are some breeds which are born without horns.

Cattle spend most of the day chewing grass. Their stomach is divided into different parts. First they swallow a lot of grass and store it in one part of the stomach. Later the grass is returned to the mouth to be chewed as cud.

CAVEMEN Long before men learned to read and write, people lived in caves. We know about cavemen from the tools they left behind them and the pictures they painted.

Cavemen hardened the points of wooden spears in a fire and made stone tools. They hunted animals for food. The women made clothes from animal hides dried in the sun. They used needles made of bone to sew the clothes together

Cavemen were hunters. At first they hunted animals with wooden spears. Sometimes the tips of the spears were hardened in a fire. Later, sharp stones were tied onto the end of the spears. No one knows who invented the bow and arrow, but it must have made hunting much easier.

Many of the simple tools the cavemen used were made from flint. Flint is a hard rock. When it is chipped it is as sharp as broken glass. The tools were used for scraping skins and carving wood. Needles for sewing animal skins together were made from the bones of animals.

People lived in caves for many thousands of years. Then they learned to grow crops and keep animals. They discovered how to get metals from the ground and how to make tools from them. People began to build houses near their fields to live in.

CENTIPEDES AND MILLIPEDES The word centipede means one hundred legs. The word millipede means one thousand legs. Both centipedes and millipedes do have a lot of legs, but centipedes often have more than one hundred legs and millipedes never have as many as one thousand legs.

Centipedes and millipedes are small animals with long bodies made up of many sections. Nearly every section of a centipede's body has one pair of legs. Nearly every section of a millipede's body has two pairs of legs. Centipedes have jaws and a pair of poison claws. They eat small insects and worms. They cannot harm people. Millipedes live on plant food.

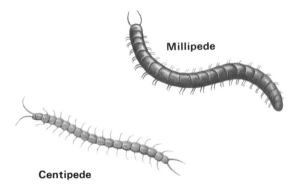

Millipede

Centipede

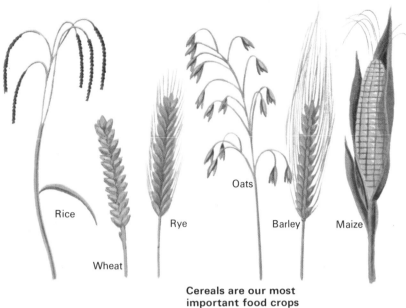

Cereals are our most important food crops

many places. Most of our flour and bread is made from wheat grain. Maize is also called corn. Maize bears its grain as long, yellow cobs. Barley and oats grow in cooler lands. They are often used for making animal foods. Millet and rye are sometimes used for making bread. Millet grows well in hot, dry lands. Rye grows where it is too cold for the other cereals to grow.

The cheetah can run faster than any other animal

CEREALS Barley, maize, millet, oats, rice, rye and wheat are all grasses. They are grown by farmers for the seeds they make. The seeds are called grain. The plants are called cereals.

Some grain is eaten whole. Rice grain is the most important food in some parts of the world. Bread is made from rye and wheat flour. Breakfast foods, cakes, pastries and animal foods are also made from cereals.

Rice grows in hot, wet lands. Most rice is grown in Asia. Wheat can be grown in

CHEETAH The cheetah belongs to the cat family. It has long legs and a small head. Like all cats, the cheetah hunts for its food. But the cheetah hunts in a different way from other cats. Instead of creeping towards an animal and then leaping upon it, the cheetah chases its prey.

The cheetah is well suited to this way of hunting. It can run faster than any other

animal. Even the swift antelope is no match for a cheetah. The only chance an antelope has of escaping is to get a good start. The cheetah tires quickly and soon gives up the chase.

CIRCUS When people think of a circus, they think of jugglers, acrobats, clowns and wild animals performing in a ring. This kind of circus is popular all over the world. But the first circuses were very different.

In the time of the Romans the circus was a place where chariots raced. The chariots were pulled by two or four horses. They were driven seven times round the track by charioteers. The charioteers needed great skill and courage to turn the sharp bends at either end of the track.

CLOCKS Long before clocks were invented, men had found ways of telling the time of day. The easiest way was the position of the Sun in the sky. Then people noticed that the shadow of a tree moved round in a half circle during the day as the Sun crossed the sky. This was how the sundial was invented. People also used sand glasses rather like egg timers to measure the passing of time.

The first real clocks were driven by weights. The weights were on a rope wound

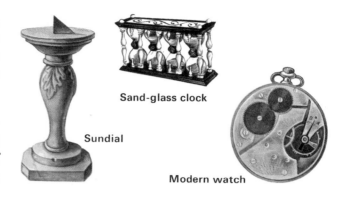

Sand-glass clock

Sundial

Modern watch

round a drum. As the rope unwound the drum turned and struck a bell every hour. When the weights reached the floor the rope was wound back on the drum.

Soon afterwards the coiled spring was invented to drive clocks. Most clocks and watches today are driven by a coiled spring.

All clocks must have something which makes sure they unwind little by little. This is called an escapement. Clocks driven by weights often have a swinging pendulum. Each time the pendulum swings from side to side it lets the weight drop a short way. Clocks driven by a spring have a small wheel which turns to and fro. At the end of each turn it lets the spring unwind a little.

Today there are many different kinds of clocks and watches. Some are driven by electricity. Some watches wind themselves up. Some clocks are so accurate that they never need to be altered.

Chariots race in a Roman circus

The highest clouds are called cirrus. They are made of ice crystals

Thunder clouds are called cumulonimbus. They are big and black

Round fluffy clouds are called cumulus. They can often be seen in the sky on a summer day

Clouds which cover the sky like a grey blanket are called stratus. Stratus clouds often bring rain

CLOUDS When wet clothes are hung on a line the sun soon dries them. The water turns to vapour and disappears into the air. The sun shining on the sea turns a lot of water to vapour all the time.

When water vapour cools it turns back to water. When vapour cools high in the sky it makes clouds. Clouds are made of millions of little drops of water. The drops are so small and so light that they stay up in the air.

If the air gets colder and colder more and more vapour turns back to water. Then the drops of water in the cloud grow bigger. They become too heavy to float in the air. They fall to the ground as raindrops. When the air is very cold the water vapour turns to ice crystals.

COAL The coal we burn for heat and power is the remains of plants which lived many millions of years ago. At that time large parts of the world were covered with swamps in which ferns grew as tall as trees. When the plants died they fell into the swamps. More plants grew and died and were buried in the mud. They sank deeper and deeper under the ground. Very slowly the mud turned into solid rock and the plant remains became coal.

Today some coal is found near the surface of the ground. But most coal is mined deep underground. In a coal mine big machines rip out the coal. The coal is carried by moving belts and railway trucks to the main shaft. There it is lifted to the surface.

Great care must be taken in mines to prevent accidents. Air in the tunnels must often be tested in case of dangerous gases. The tunnels must be supported with steel or concrete beams to make sure they do not collapse. And miners must take great care to guard against fire.

Most of the coal mined is burned in power stations or in the home. Some is made into coke and coal gas. Perfumes, dyes, plastics and fertilizers can also be made from coal.

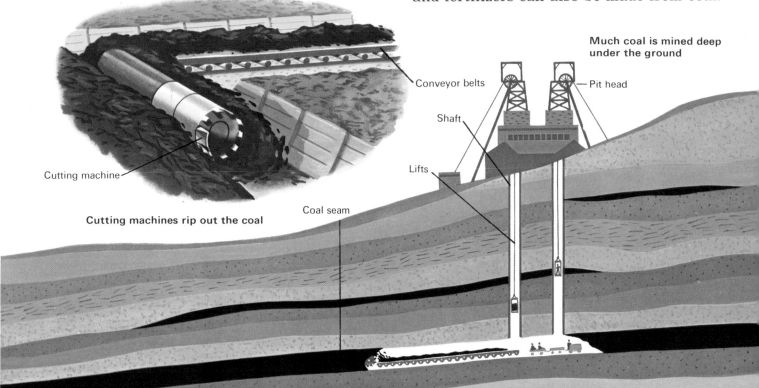
Cutting machine

Cutting machines rip out the coal

Coal seam

Much coal is mined deep under the ground

Conveyor belts

Pit head

Shaft

Lifts

COLOUR Sunlight is made up of light of many different colours. This can be seen when sunlight passes through a prism. A prism is a piece of glass shaped rather like the roof of a house. A prism splits sunlight up into its various colours. This range of colours is called the spectrum. The colours of the spectrum are red, orange, yellow, green, blue, indigo and violet. If lights of these different colours are mixed together, they make white light again.

A comet often has a long, bright tail

Blue, red and yellow paints can be mixed together to make all other colours

Grass is green and daffodils are yellow because they take in, or absorb, some of the colours of sunlight. Grass absorbs all colours but green. Green light is reflected into our eyes. Daffodils absorb all colours but yellow. Yellow light is reflected into our eyes. Things which reflect all the colours of sunlight appear white. Things which absorb all the colours of sunlight appear black.

If two paints of different colours are mixed together, they make a new colour. Red and yellow make orange. Blue and red make purple. Blue and yellow make green. If paints of all these colours are mixed together the mixture is black. No light is being reflected into our eyes.

COMET A comet is a ball of dust and gas which travels through space round the Sun. At night a comet appears as a bright ball of light with a glowing tail. The Sun's rays make the gas in the comet glow.

People used to think that a comet in the sky was a warning of a tragedy on Earth. Now scientists can tell exactly when comets will appear. The most famous is Halley's comet. It was last seen in 1910 and is expected to return in 1986.

COMPASS For hundreds of years people have used a compass to find their way across the land and the sea. The compass is an instrument which shows the direction of North.

The simplest compass is a magnet which is able to spin round. The magnet will always come to rest pointing North.

The magnetic compass is very useful, but it is not very accurate. Ships and planes now have gyrocompasses. A gyrocompass has a spinning wheel which always stays in the same position, no matter how the ship or plane twists and turns.

When a compass needle spins round it comes to rest with one end pointing north

COMPUTER A spacecraft carrying astronauts to the Moon travels at about six thousand miles an hour. The spacecraft's retrorockets must be fired at exactly the right moment to put the craft in orbit round the Moon. If the rockets are not fired at the right time, the spacecraft will either crash into the moon or speed past it and be lost in space.

How do the astronauts know the exact moment to fire the rockets? A computer tells them. Only a computer could work out all the calculations quickly enough. Computers control almost every move on a space mission, from launch to splash-down.

A computer is simply a very fast calculating machine. In a fraction of a second it can work out sums that would take men days to do. And computers cannot make mistakes. Computers are used today for many things from working out people's wages to producing weather forecasts.

The orang utan is a shy animal which lives in the forests of Indonesia. So many orang utans have been captured for zoos that there are very few left in the wild. These animals are now protected but there are many other animals which will soon exist only in zoos unless people stop hunting and trapping them

CONSERVATION For hundreds of years men have been destroying the world of nature. Forests have been chopped down to make way for farms and factories. The waste from factories has poisoned, or polluted, lakes and rivers. And many animals are in danger of becoming extinct. Conservation is the protection of nature. It is something which concerns everyone.

The pollution of the air and the sea is one of the biggest problems. Fumes from factories and cars are making the air dirtier than ever before. Chemicals from factories and oil from tankers are poisoning lakes and seas. Many scientists are working out ways of stopping this pollution.

Many people are also trying to save the wildlife of the world. So many animals have been killed for their skins or captured for zoos that many kinds are in danger of becoming extinct. Now some countries have put aside land where the animals can live in peace.

Creatures which live in the sea also need protection. Unless people stop hunting the blue whale there will be none left in a few years time. The biggest animal ever to live on the Earth will have become extinct. It will have been killed by man.

Corals grow in beautiful shapes

CORAL Many ships have been sunk on coral reefs. Coral reefs are jagged ridges of rock just below the surface of the sea. They are found only in warm waters.

It seems hard to believe that coral reefs are built by animals. They are made of the skeletons of millions of tiny animals called coral polyps. Coral polyps are like little blobs of jelly. Each polyp builds a hard case or skeleton around itself. When the polyp dies the skeleton remains. More and more polyps build their skeletons on top of the old ones, and so the reef grows. Near Australia there is a coral reef more than one thousand miles long.

Costume has changed greatly over the centuries

3,000 years ago   2,000 years ago   300 years ago   200 years ago   100 years ago   60 years ago   40 years ago   Present day

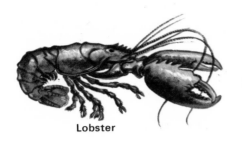
Lobster

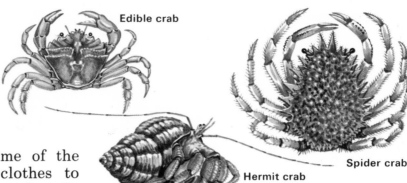
Edible crab

Spider crab

Hermit crab

COSTUME Ever since the time of the cavemen people have worn clothes to protect themselves from the weather. In some parts of the world it is so hot that people need very few clothes. In other parts of the world it is so cold that every part of the body must be covered by thick furs. Many different clothes are worn in different parts of the world.

In most parts of the world people's dress, or costume, has changed a great deal over the years. The clothes we wear are different from the clothes our grandparents wore, and they are quite different from the clothes people wore hundreds of years ago.

In some countries people still wear 'national costume' for special occasions. This is the costume which has been worn for hundreds of years in those countries.

Crocodile

CRABS Crabs belong to the groups of animals called crustaceans. They are relatives of shrimps and lobsters. Like all crustaceans, crabs have a hard shell, or skeleton, on the outside of their body, and jointed legs. Most crabs also have strong claws or pincers.

Most crabs live in the sea. They move over the sea-bed in a curious sideways walk looking for scraps of food. Some crabs are good swimmers. The swimming crabs use their feathery back legs as oars.

There are many different kinds of crabs. One of the strangest is the hermit crab. Hermit crabs do not have a hard shell on their body. Instead they find an empty sea-shell in which to live.

CROCODILES Crocodiles are large reptiles which live in rivers and swamps in hot lands. They have a long tail, short legs and powerful jaws with sharp teeth. Crocodiles spend much of their time basking in the sun or floating in the water with their eyes and nostrils just above the surface.

CRUSADES The word crusade means war of the cross. The Crusades were fought many years ago between Christian knights and the Turks. The Turks were not Christians. They were followers of Mohammed. The Crusaders were fighting to take the Holy Land from the Turks.

Knight Templar

During the Crusades some knights formed groups called Orders. The Templars, Hospitallers and the Teutonic Knights from Germany were the most important. They helped Christian pilgrims travelling to the Holy Land and protected them from the Turks

Teutonic Knight

At first the Crusaders were successful. They captured many parts of the Holy Land. When they went into battle they felt they were fighting for God. They wore a cross for their badge and shouted 'Deus Vult' meaning 'God wills it' as their battle cry. The most famous Crusader was King Richard the Lionheart.

The cuckoo lays its eggs in other birds' nests

The young cuckoo may be larger than its foster mother

CUCKOO The cuckoo is well-known for its strange call. It is heard far more often than it is seen. The cuckoo is also well-known for the way it lays its eggs in the nests of other birds. A female cuckoo lays only one egg in each nest. Her egg is often much bigger than the eggs already there, but the mother bird does not notice.

When the eggs hatch the young cuckoo pushes the other chicks out of the nest. The foster parents feed the cuckoo until it is fully grown. Sometimes the young cuckoo may be three times as big as the birds which are feeding it.

Cuckoos fly to warm lands for the winter. They fly back to cooler lands in spring. Many people listen for the first call of the cuckoo. It is a sign that winter is over. Only the male bird sings 'cuckoo'.

The water held back by a dam can be used to drive machines which make electricity

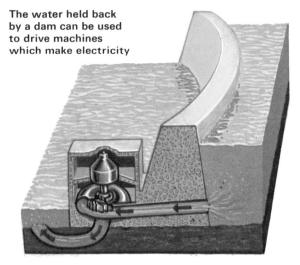

DAMS A lot of water is used in homes and factories. Much is also needed to grow crops in dry lands. Water must be stored to make sure there is always enough, even when the weather is dry.

The best way of storing water is to build a wall across a river. The wall is called a dam. The river turns into a big lake behind a dam. Water can be taken from the lake as it is needed. The water can also be used to drive big machines which produce electricity.

Dams must be very large and very strong to hold back a river. The biggest dams are made of steel and concrete. Their curved shape gives them extra strength.

DEEP-SEA FISHES Deep down in the sea it is very dark and the water is icy cold. This is the home of many strange fishes. Most deep-sea fishes can make their own light. They have lights arranged in patterns along their bodies. The lights help them to find mates and food in the darkness.

Plants do not grow deep under the sea, so deep-sea fishes feed upon each other and upon dead animals which fall to the sea bed. Most of these fishes have huge teeth and some eat animals larger than themselves.

Deep-sea fishes look very fierce but most of them are no bigger than your thumb

One of the strangest deep-sea fishes is the angler fish. It has a light above its mouth which can be switched on and off. Any fish which is attracted towards the light is swallowed in one gulp.

The bodies of deep-sea fishes are built to withstand the tremendous weight of all the water above them. They die if they are brought to the surface of the sea.

DEER There are many kinds of deer. They are hoofed animals which can run quickly and jump gracefully. Male deer have branching antlers made of bone. A new pair of antlers is grown every spring. At first the antlers are covered with soft skin like velvet. As the antlers grow the skin peels off.

The spadefoot toad lives in the desert but it does not like the sun. So it digs a hole in the sand with its back feet and buries itself.

The biggest deer are the American moose and the European elk. They are taller than a man. Most common is the shy red deer which lives in the woodlands of Europe and North America. The smallest deer is the chevrotain. It is only two feet long. The chevrotain lives in the forests of South-East Asia.

Male deer fight with their antlers in the mating season

DESERTS Those parts of the world which have very little rain are called deserts. There are big deserts in every continent except Europe. Some deserts are made of sand dunes. Others are bare rock.

Deserts are not easy places for plants and animals to live in. During the day it is very hot. At night it can be bitterly cold. Sometimes years may pass without a single drop of rain falling. Then there will be a storm which floods the land. There are also sandstorms which may last for days on end.

The jerboa is a rodent with long back legs which lives in the desert. It comes out at night and hops over the sand looking for food. There are similar animals in most deserts

During the day a desert seems a deserted place. The animals which live there hide from the sun. They come out at night to look for food. There are lizards, snakes, scorpions and small rat-like animals with long back legs. These small animals get nearly all the water from the food they eat.

Although there is little rain, plants manage to live in the desert. Some have long roots which reach deep into the ground to soak up water. Others have ways of storing

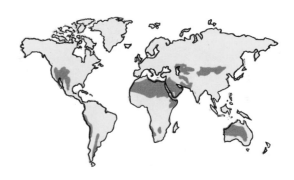

The deserts of the world

water in their stems. Most desert plants are prickly. This prevents them being eaten by the desert animals for the water they hold.

After a shower of rain the desert is covered by a carpet of small, bright flowers. The seeds may have been lying for years in the sand waiting for rain.

Few people live in deserts. In some places there are waterholes called oases where people can grow crops. Other people roam the desert with flocks of camels, sheep, or goats, looking for patches of grass.

Tyrannosaurus, a meat-eating dinosaur

Allosaurus, a meat-eating dinosaur

Early reptile

DINOSAUR Many millions of years ago, reptiles ruled the world. There were reptiles on the land, reptiles in the sea, and reptiles in the air. The biggest of the reptiles were the dinosaurs.

The name dinosaur means 'terrible lizard'. Some of the dinosaurs were the biggest animals ever to live on the land. Brachiosaurus was the giant of them all. It was as heavy as ten elephants. Brontosaurus was also huge. From the tip of its long tail to the front of its tiny head, Brontosaurus measured over seventy feet.

The largest dinosaurs were peaceful creatures. They spent most of their time in swamps and lakes eating plants. They had to eat all day long to get enough food for their huge bodies.

The greatest enemy of the plant-eating dinosaurs was Tyrannosaurus Rex. Its name means 'King of Tyrants'. Tyrannosaurus had huge jaws with long, sharp teeth. It walked on its back legs which were as thick as tree trunks. Its front legs were tiny and of no use.

Some dinosaurs could run fast enough to escape Tyrannosaurus. Others had bony armour to protect them. Triceratops had great bony horns on its head. Stegosaurus had a long spiked tail which it could swing like a club.

No one has ever seen a dinosaur. Only their skeletons remain in the rocks. Their skeletons show that dinosaurs were stupid animals. The very largest had a brain the size of a hen's egg.

Some of the dinosaurs were the largest animals ever to live on the land. The very biggest were harmless plant eating animals. The dreaded enemy of the plant eating dinosaurs was Tyrannosaurus. Not all of the animals in the picture lived at the same time

Pteranodon, a flying reptile

Brontosaurus, a plant-eating dinosaur

Triceratops, a plant-eating dinosaur

Early amphibian

C. HOWELL-JONES. 72.

Dodo

DODO People are sometimes said to be 'as silly as a dodo'. The dodo was a flightless bird which once lived on a few islands. The dodo was no sillier than other birds, except for one thing. It was not scared of people. When sailors came to the islands the dodo did not run away. Soon they had all been killed for food.

DOGS The dog is often called 'man's best friend'. Dogs can be trained to help people in many ways, including hunting, herding farm animals, keeping guard, guiding blind people, and pulling sledges.

Dogs that help men hunt are called sporting dogs. They include terriers, hounds, spaniels, setters, pointers and retrievers. Other dogs that help men are called working dogs. Sheepdogs round up sheep. Huskies pull sledges across the snow. The St Bernard is well known for its rescue work in mountains. And various dogs such as the Alsatian are used as guard dogs.

Many other breeds of dogs are kept as pets. They include toy dogs which are the smallest breeds. Smallest of all is the chihuahua. It is small enough to sit on a person's hand.

Domestic dogs belong to the same family of animals as the wolf, jackal and fox. Dogs are meat-eaters. Together with cats, dogs are the best hunters among animals.

DRAGONFLY The dragonfly is an insect with a long colourful body and four large, gauzy wings. It can be seen flitting over ponds and rivers in the summer.

Dragonflies can fly very well. They can dart through the air faster than other insects. They can hover like a helicopter. They can even fly backwards. Dragonflies feed on other insects which they catch in the air.

Dragonfly

DUCKS The duck family includes ducks, swans and geese. They are all swimming birds with short legs and webbed feet. Some ducks have broad, flat beaks which they use to sift worms and other small animals from the mud and water. The best sifting beak belongs to the shoveller duck. It is fringed with small plates like bristles. The plates hold back pieces of food when the mud and water are squeezed out of the beak. Other ducks have sharp beaks and dive under water for their food. Many ducks have gaily coloured feathers.

Police dog

Sheepdog

Guide dog

The duck family includes many different birds

Swans are the largest birds of the duck family. They have slender necks which are longer than their bodies. Swans are so heavy that they must paddle some way through the water before they can take-off. A male swan is called a cob. A female swan is called a pen. Young swans are called cygnets. Some swans are snowy-white with black feathers on their head and a bright orange beak. Other swans are black. Black swans live in Australia.

Geese are smaller than swans but larger than ducks. There are many different kinds living in different parts of the world. One of the best known is the Canada goose. It spends the summer in cold lands and flies to warmer lands for the winter. Canada geese fly together in V shaped groups. The word goose is really the name of the female bird. A male goose is called a gander.

Eagles have a sharp, hooked beak for tearing flesh and strong talons for grasping their prey

EAGLES Eagles are large, fierce birds. Some eagles are so large that with out-spread wings they would stretch from one end of a bed to the other. Eagles eat small animals so they are called birds of prey. They catch their prey in their huge claws and fly away with it. Some eagles are so strong that they can carry off lambs and young deer.

Eagles live in many parts of the world. They build nests in the tops of tall trees and on cliffs. These nests are called eyries. Once there were many eagles. Today there are not many eagles left.

EAR We hear sounds with our ears. Sounds are really vibrations or 'shakings' of the air. Our ears pick up these vibrations and pass signals about them to our brain.

The ear has three parts. The outer ear has an ear flap to pick up the vibrations of the air and an ear passage. At the end of the ear passage is the ear drum. This is just like a drum skin. The vibrations of the air pass down the ear passage and make the ear drum vibrate.

In the middle ear are little bones. They pass the vibrations of the ear drum to the inner ear. The inner ear has coiled tubes filled with liquid. The vibrations make the liquid vibrate and tiny hairs send signals to our brain. Our brain turns the signals into sounds.

The inner ear has other tubes filled with liquid called semi-circular canals. These help us to keep our balance. As we move the liquid in the semi-circular canals moves too. Tiny hairs in the liquid send signals to the brain about the movement. This is how we can tell when we are standing upright even with our eyes closed.

Diagram of an ear

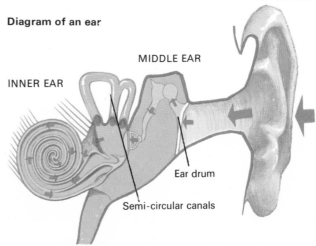

OUTER EAR

MIDDLE EAR

INNER EAR

Ear drum

Semi-circular canals

The centre of the Earth is a hot ball of molten metal

EARTH The Earth is the planet we live on. It is one of nine planets which travel through space round the Sun. Some of the other planets are larger than the Earth. And most are farther away from the Sun.

The time the Earth takes to travel once round the sun is called a year. The Earth also spins around as it travels through space. The time the Earth takes to spin once is called a day.

The Earth is a great ball of rock. The lightest rocks are on the outside. They make the continents and the floor of the sea. This is called the crust of the Earth. Beneath the crust are heavier rocks. No one can be sure what the middle of the Earth is like. Many scientists believe it may be a huge lump of molten metal.

The Earth is the only planet with water. And it is the only planet surrounded by air.

Many scientists believe that the Earth and the other planets came from the Sun. They believe that the Earth began as a great cloud of dust and gas. The specks of dust and gas slowly came together to make a solid planet.

EARTHQUAKE The ground under our feet feels very solid. It is made of rock. But sometimes the rock breaks and moves. When this happens the ground shakes. This is called an earthquake.

In some parts of the world there are many earthquakes. Most of them are too small to be noticed except by special instruments. Very occasionally there is a big earthquake. Then the ground shakes hard. Buildings fall down and great gaps open in the ground. Many people have died in earthquakes. Many more have been left homeless.

Scientists know where big earthquakes are likely to happen. But they do not know yet when they will happen. In places where there are many earthquakes tall buildings are made so that they will not fall down when the ground shakes.

ECLIPSE As the Moon travels through space round the Earth it sometimes passes between the Earth and the Sun. The Moon blots out the Sun's rays and the day grows dark. This is called a solar eclipse. At other times the Earth comes between the Sun and the Moon. The Earth blots out the Sun's rays and the Moon grows dim. This is called a lunar eclipse.

It took thousands of slaves and many years to build the great pyramids of Egypt

During an eclipse the Sun or Moon is not always completely hidden. Scientists know all about the movements of the Earth and the Moon. They can tell when an eclipse will take place.

The fierce Moray eel feeds on octopuses

EEL An eel looks rather like a snake. But it is really a fish. The eels found in the rivers of Europe and North America begin their life in the sea. They hatch from eggs laid in parts of the Atlantic Ocean. It may take the young eels three years to find their way across the sea to the rivers of Europe.

When they reach the rivers the males stay near the coast, but the females swim far upstream. They live in the rivers for some years. Then they swim back to where they were born to lay their eggs. Soon afterwards they die.

EGYPT, ANCIENT The magnificent civilisation of the ancient Egyptians grew up along the banks of the river Nile thousands of years ago. Each year the Nile flooded leaving a layer of rich soil. Egyptian farmers planted their crops in this soil. They also built networks of canals to water the land.

Egypt was ruled by pharaohs. The ruling pharaoh was both a god and king to his people. The pharaohs employed thousands

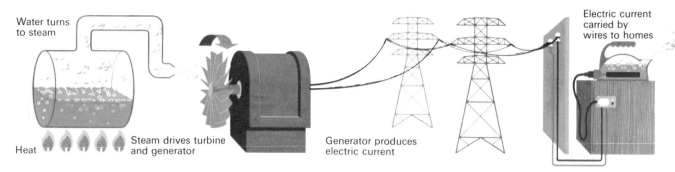

Water turns to steam

Heat

Steam drives turbine and generator

Generator produces electric current

Electric current carried by wires to homes

of people—priests and scribes (people who could write), craftsmen and artists, as well as sculptors and builders.

Egyptian buildings and art were mainly for the dead. And they were made to last for ever. The pharaohs and nobles were buried in vast stone tombs called pyramids. The Egyptians believed that after death the soul would return to live in the body. So they took great care to preserve the body.

The Egyptians were good mathematicians. They were also skilled astronomers and were among the first surgeons. The Egyptians developed a form of writing called hieroglyphs. Hieroglyphs are picture writing. Each picture stands for a word or an idea.

ELECTRICITY All materials are made of tiny particles called atoms. Atoms contain even tinier particles called electrons. In some materials a few electrons in each atom are only loosely held. These are called free electrons. They can jump from atom to atom. A movement of electrons from atom to atom is called electricity.

An electric current is a flow of free electrons along a wire. The electrons are made to flow in one direction by making sure that atoms at one end of the wire are short of electrons while atoms at the other end of the wire have too many. This difference is called an electrical pressure, or voltage.

A current of electricity must have a completely unbroken path, or circuit. If we could follow a current as it flowed along a wire we would arrive back at our starting point.

Wires which carry an electric current are often made of copper. Copper, like other metals, is a good conductor of electricity. It has a lot of free electrons. Materials like rubber and plastic are bad conductors of electricity. They have no free electrons.

How electricity comes to the home

Bad conductors are called insulators.

When an electric current passes through a wire, the wire becomes hot. The thinner the wire the hotter it becomes. Very thin wires become white-hot. They are used in electric lights. Wires which become red-hot are used in electric-fires.

The electricity we use in the home is made in power stations by big machines called generators. It is carried by wires to our homes where it is used for heating, lighting and cooking.

ELEMENTS Everything is made of tiny particles called atoms. There are many different kinds of atoms. The different kinds of atoms make different materials called elements. Gold is an element. So are carbon, copper, hydrogen, oxygen and many others. There are almost one hundred elements in the world.

How Eskimos live in the winter and summer

Most elements join with other elements to make compounds. Water is a compound. It is made when oxygen and hydrogen join together. There are many, many compounds.

ELEPHANT The elephant is the largest animal now living on the land. A big male elephant can weigh up to seven tons. It needs a quarter of a ton of grass and fifty gallons of water each day to feed its huge body.

Elephants can lift big logs with their trunk

The strangest thing about an elephant is its long trunk. The tip of the trunk is so sensitive that it can pick up a single peanut. The trunk is also strong enough to lift whole tree trunks. The elephant uses its trunk to gather food and suck up water. The elephant squirts the water into its mouth or over its back.

There are two kinds of elephants, African elephants and Indian elephants. The African elephant is larger than the Indian elephant and has much bigger ears.

ESKIMOS The Eskimos live in the far north. They are short people with yellow skins and black hair. Their faces are wide and rather flat. Their eyes are narrow.

For most of the year the lands where the Eskimos live are covered with snow. They travel across the snow in sledges. The sledges are pulled by strong dogs called huskies. The Eskimos hunt seals and walruses and bears. They eat the meat and use the fat in their lamps. They use the animal skins to make warm clothes. They wear strong boots, baggy trousers, and coats with hoods.

In the short summer months the Eskimos paddle through the water in canoes called kayaks. They live in wooden huts or tents of skin. In winter Eskimos build houses of snow. They are called igloos.

Now the Eskimos' way of life is changing. More and more of them are living in towns and learning modern ways of life.

Europe in pictures

Fishing

Skiing in the Alps

Europe was the home of ancient civilizations

Europe has many canals

Traditional costume

A Village

Europe has many industries

EUROPE The continent of Europe is the second smallest continent, yet no other continent has played such an important part in the history of the world. European ideas, discoveries, languages and ways of life have spread to many other parts of the world. Europe is known as the birthplace of western civilization.

For such a small continent Europe has many different kinds of scenery. There are huge forests, fertile plains and high mountains. Europe has many large rivers. Most are used for carrying goods. They are linked to one another by canals.

Most of Europe has a mild climate. In winter winds blowing from the Atlantic Ocean warm large parts of the continent. During summer the same winds keep the continent cool. These winds bring rain at all times of the year. Few parts of Europe suffer from a lack of water.

Most European farms are small but well run. Farm workers make up one-third of Europe's people. They grow many crops including wheat, potatoes, sugar beet, vegetables and grapes among many others.

Although the farmers get very big crops from the land there are so many people living in Europe that few countries can produce all the food they need. Instead, Europe has many factories making all kinds of goods which are sold to the rest of the world. These goods help pay for the food which has to be bought from other countries. More than half the world's iron and coal are mined in Europe.

The people of Europe are made up of many different nationalities. Each has its own language and way of life. Some of the nations of Europe have joined together to form the European Economic Community. More and more countries are joining the Community. The aim of the Community is to make a United States of Europe in which all the countries work together and help each other.

EVOLUTION Millions of years ago the horse was the size of a large dog and had five toes on each foot. As time went by horses grew in size and had fewer toes on each foot. Today the horse has only one toe or hoof on each foot. The horse has changed, or evolved, over millions of years.

44

Known world
1550

1850

1900

Most scientists believe that evolution explains how all the different plants and animals came into being. They believe that the first living things were microscopic forms of life. Very slowly these simple forms of life evolved into bigger and more complicated plants and animals. Fishes evolved from small sea creatures, amphibians evolved from fishes, reptiles evolved from amphibians, and birds and mammals evolved from reptiles.

Scientists believe that evolution happens because no two animals are exactly the same. Because they are slightly different, one animal will be better able to survive than another. For instance, one animal may be able to run faster to escape its enemies than another animal of the same kind. Its young will also be able to run faster. After a long time the animals which can run faster may be the only ones left of that kind of animal.

EXPLORATION Men have always been curious. They have wanted to find out about far off places and see how other people live. So for hundreds of years men have explored the world.

Exploration is a very dangerous business. The early explorers set out in small wooden ships. They could not carry much food. They sailed across vast oceans and were buffeted by terrible storms. They did not know when they would reach land. And they did not know what the land would be like when they did reach it. Perhaps the people living there would be unfriendly. They might have to hack their way through dense forests or jungles. They might have to plod across deserts which seemed endless.

Today almost all the world has been explored. But men are still curious about their surroundings. So now men are starting to explore space.

Some famous moments in the story of exploration

Columbus discovers the New World

Sturt crosses Australia

Scott reaches the South Pole just after the Norwegian explorer Amundsen

Lewis and Clark cross the Rockies

Livingstone discovers the Victoria Falls

Magellan sails round Cape Horn

The eyes of insects are made up of thousands of small eyes. They are called compound eyes

EYE Our eyes are very much like a camera. In the centre of each eye there is a black circle called a pupil. This lets light into the eye. Behind the pupil is a lens. The lens throws a picture of what is in front of it onto the retina at the back of the eye. A nerve runs from the retina to the brain. Whenever a picture is thrown on the retina, the nerve carries a message to the brain. The brain translates the message back into a picture and we 'see'.

The coloured part of the eye is called the iris. It is a ring of muscle that makes the pupil larger or smaller. In bright light the pupil gets smaller. In dim light it gets larger to let more light into the eye.

Many animals have eyes like our own. But some animals have simpler eyes, and some cannot see at all. The strangest eyes belong to the insects. They are made up of thousands of small eyes.

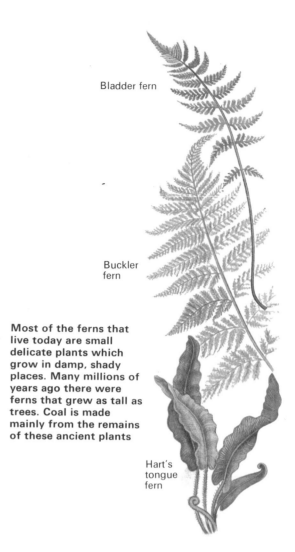

Bladder fern

Buckler fern

Most of the ferns that live today are small delicate plants which grow in damp, shady places. Many millions of years ago there were ferns that grew as tall as trees. Coal is made mainly from the remains of these ancient plants

Hart's tongue fern

Farmers use many machines. One of the useful machines on a farm is the tractor

FARMING We must all eat to live, to work, and to enjoy life. Thousands of years ago Man could only get food by hunting animals and picking wild fruits. Later, he learnt to grow crops and to raise animals for their milk, meat, and eggs. He became a farmer.

Today we all depend on farmers for nearly everything we eat. Farming is the world's largest and most important industry.

For hundreds of years methods of farming changed very little. Up to a very few years ago most farms in Britain and other parts of the world were mixed farms. The mixed farmer grew corn and root crops. He also raised livestock. He kept some cattle for milk, others for beef. He might also keep pigs. And on rough pastures he would allow sheep to graze.

Today most farmers specialize. The arable farmer grows only crops. The dairy farmer earns a living from his milking cows. It is the same with the pig farmer, sheep farmer and poultry farmer.

The other great change that has happened in farming is that it has become mechanized. Many jobs once done by hand or with animals are now done with machines. Tractors now pull the plough instead of horses or oxen. The combine-harvester cuts and threshes corn in one go. It even puts the grain into sacks to be stored. Today cows are milked by machine and sheep are sheared with electric shearers.

FERNS Millions of years ago ferns were the most important plants in the world. Some ferns grew as tall as trees. Others made a carpet over the ground like grass does now. Today there are far fewer ferns. They are mostly small, delicate plants which live in damp places.

Ferns grow from spores which are formed in small brown cases either under the leaves or on special stems. The spores do not grow into plants which look like their parents. Instead they grow into heart-shaped plants about the size of a thumbnail. It is these which produce the normal fern plants.

FINGERPRINTS If you look at the tips of your fingers you can see little ridges on the skin. These ridges make patterns of loops. There is no one else in the world whose fingers have exactly the same pattern on them as yours.

When you touch something your fingers leave marks on it. These marks are called fingerprints. They are very useful to the police. After a crime they look at everything the criminal might have touched. He may have left fingerprints. Many criminals have been caught because of the fingerprints they left behind them.

FISH There are more kinds of fishes than there are of amphibians, reptiles, birds and mammals put together. Some fishes live in the sea. Some live in fresh water. And some

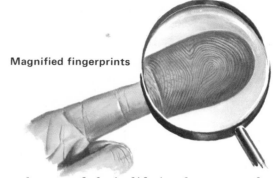

Magnified fingerprints

spend part of their life in the sea and part in fresh water.

A fish swims through the water by bending its body to and fro and by moving its tail. Fins help it to keep upright and to move up or down. The fins also act as brakes.

Most fishes are covered by scales. Some fishes have a special line of scales down the middle of their body. They help the fish to sense vibrations in the water.

Fishes need oxygen just as land animals do. But fishes do not have lungs. Instead they breathe with gills.

Almost all fishes hatch from eggs. Some fishes lay millions of eggs and leave them to float in the water. Few of the eggs survive. If they did the oceans would soon be full of fish. Other fishes lay fewer eggs but take more care of them. Some sticklebacks build nests for their eggs and the male keeps guard over it. The male seahorse carries the eggs in a pouch on his body. Some fishes even carry the eggs in their mouth. When the young fishes hatch they swim near the mother. At the first sign of danger they dart back into her mouth.

Many fishes have strange habits. The flying fish can glide a long way over the waves using its fins as wings. The archer fish catches insects by squirting water at them.

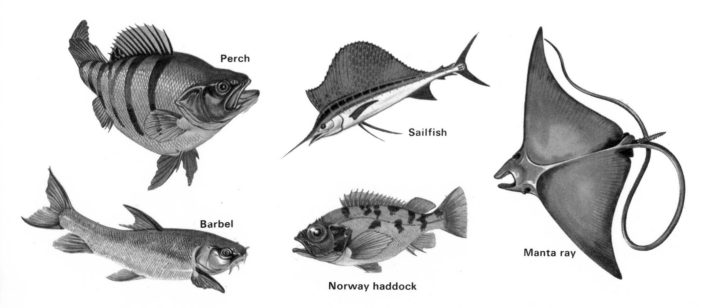

Perch

Sailfish

Barbel

Norway haddock

Manta ray

FLAG The ancient Egyptians were the first people to fly flaglike streamers. These were attached to long poles or *standards*, and were used in battle. This custom continued throughout history. Each side had its *standard-bearer*, who held the standard high for all to see. It helped soldiers to find their comrades quickly.

Flags have always been important as a means of identifying ships. Sailors also use flags for sending messages in the International Flag Code.

The most familiar flags in the modern world are those of nations and of international organizations such as the United Nations and the Red Cross. Most of these are oblong in shape.

FLOWERS Everywhere you go, you see flowers growing. They grow in gardens, in fields and in hedges. They grow in deserts, in marshes and even in rivers and ponds. There are thousands and thousands of different kinds. Some are tiny weeds. Others are great trees like the oak. Some have beautiful flowers like the rose. Others, like grass, have flowers that are too small and dull to be noticed.

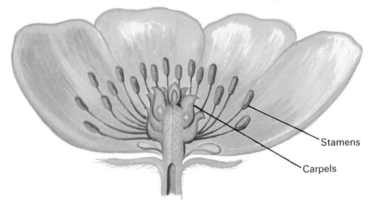

A flower cut away to show its parts

Stamens

Carpels

Almost every flowering plant starts its life as a seed lying in the ground. When the weather turns warm in spring, the hard case of the seed splits and the plant starts to grow, using food stored in the seed. It puts out roots which take in moisture and special salts from the soil. Its shoot grows up to the surface and its new leaves unfold.

The plant breathes through its leaves. It also uses its leaves to make food. They take in a gas from the air called carbon dioxide. With this and the water from the roots, the

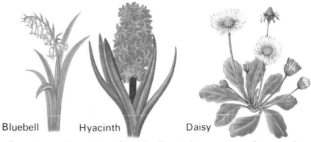

Some of the different shapes of flower heads

Bluebell   Hyacinth   Daisy

plant makes its food. But it can only make food in the sunlight. There is a special green stuff in the leaves, called chlorophyll. The chlorophyll uses the sunlight to turn the water and gas into food.

When the plant is fully grown its flowers come out. Inside the pretty petals there are

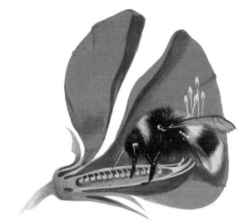

Bees carry pollen from flower to flower as they feed on nectar at the bottom of the petals

stamens and carpels. New seeds are made in the carpels. Before the seeds can be made, the carpels must be brushed with pollen from the stamens of another flower. Sometimes pollen is carried from flower to flower by insects. Sometimes it is blown by the wind. Insects do not mean to pollinate flowers. They visit them to feed on the nectar at the bottom of the petals. As they reach into the flowers the pollen clings to their bodies. When they move to a new flower the pollen is brushed on to the carpels. When the flower has been pollinated the new seeds grow. The flowers die down and the carpels grow into fruits. The fruits cover the seeds and protect them until they are ready to grow into new plants.

FLIES Of all the nasty insect pests, flies are the most dangerous. They spread all kinds of germs and diseases. The housefly picks up germs as it buzzes round rubbish dumps and may carry them to our food. In

Brier rose   African lily

FOG Air contains water in the form of invisible vapour. Warm air can hold more water vapour than cold air. When air cools, some of the vapour turns back into tiny water droplets. The droplets are so light they float in the air.

When water droplets appear high in the sky they make clouds. When water droplets appear near the ground they make fog. Fog forms when warm, moist air passes over cold ground or water and is chilled.

hot countries flies carry some of the worst diseases. The mosquito carries malaria and yellow fever. The tsetse fly carries sleeping sickness. Other kinds of flies suck the blood of cattle or lay their eggs in the skin of animals.

Houseflies taste with their feet. They cannot bite or pierce food. They have to pour a special juice on the food to dissolve it. They suck up the liquid with their mouths.

FOSSIL The remains or traces of plants and animals which lived many millions of years ago are called fossils. A fossil may be a shell, a tooth, or a skeleton. It may be a footprint or the shape of a leaf on a rock. Sometimes animals are found preserved exactly as they were in life. In very cold lands mammoths have been found in ice. The ice has preserved them like a refrigerator.

Most fossils are the remains of sea animals. When these creatures die they sink to the sea bed and their shells and skeletons are covered by mud. The mud becomes layers of rock and the shells and bones are petrified. The word petrified means 'turned to stone'. Much later the sea bed may become dry land. Wind and rain wear away the rocks until the fossils are uncovered.

Plants are sometimes turned into fossils when they die and fall into swamps. Coal is the remains of fern forests of long ago. Often the pattern of the fern leaves can be seen in the coal.

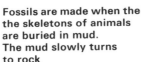

Many fossils are the remains of sea creatures

**Fossils are made when the the skeletons of animals are buried in mud.
The mud slowly turns to rock**

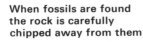

When fossils are found the rock is carefully chipped away from them

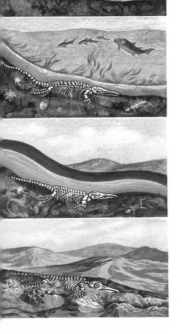

Red fox and cub

FOX All the members of the dog family are intelligent animals. But none is as cunning as the fox.

The red fox lives in forests and woods. It lives and hunts by itself. During the day it hides and sleeps in its underground den, or 'earth'. At night it hunts the small creatures that live on the forest floor. It also steals chickens and other small animals from farms.

The fox is often hunted by man, but it is so cunning that it is very hard to catch. It knows all sorts of tricks for throwing hounds and hunters off its track.

The Arctic fox lives in the far north. In winter its grey coat goes white to match the Arctic snow. The fennec fox lives in the desert. It has big, pointed ears.

FROGS AND TOADS In spring, frogs and toads lay their eggs. The frog lays its eggs in a clump in the water. The clump of jelly-covered eggs is called frog-spawn. The eggs

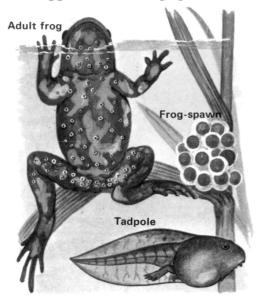

Adult frog

Frog-spawn

Tadpole

hatch into tadpoles that swim like fishes with their long tails. Gradually the tadpole grows legs and the fishy gills it was born with turn into lungs. Its tail gets shorter and shorter until it turns into a frog and hops out of the water on to the land.

On land, frogs and toads eat small insects and worms. When it sees a tasty fly, the frog shoots out its long, sticky tongue and, in a second, the fly is swallowed whole.

Tree frogs have long 'fingers' with sticky pads on them. It is very hard to see them as they climb and swing through the leaves because they are as green as the leaves themselves.

The male midwife toad carries the eggs on its back

Most of the tree frogs are safe from their enemies because they cannot be seen. Some frogs and toads can easily be seen. Their bright colours are often a warning to other animals that they are poisonous. The poisonous toads have glands full of poison behind their heads.

Breviceps is a little toad that lives in a burrow in the sand to keep cool. It digs with its back foot which is shaped like a spade. It is very shy. When it is outside its safe burrow it tries to look fierce by puffing itself up like a balloon.

FROST When warm air cools, some of the invisible water vapour it holds turns back to droplets of water. If the air becomes very cold the vapour turns to ice crystals. Frost is a layer of ice crystals which forms on the ground during a cold winter night. The ground loses much of its heat at night and chills the air lying above it. Frost also makes lacy patterns of ice crystals on cold window panes in winter.

Some of the many different kinds of fruit

Blackberry

Orange

Strawberry

Raspberry

FRUIT When people think of fruit, they think of apples, oranges, bananas, pineapples and all the other fruits in the fruit bowl. They do not think of cucumbers, walnuts and pea pods. But these are just as much fruits.

New plants grow from seeds. The seeds are made inside the carpels of the flower. The carpels turn into fruits. The fruits help to protect the seeds and to move them to new places where they will be able to grow. Some fruits, like the sycamore, have wings that carry the seeds on the wind. Others have sweet, juicy flesh which animals carry away as food.

Some fruits, such as plums and cherries, are made from just the carpels. These are called 'true' fruits. 'False' fruits are made from other parts of the plant as well. Apples and pears are made from the swollen flower stalk. The carpels and their seeds form the apple core.

Many fruits are important food crops. The apple family includes the pear, peach, plum, cherry, apricot, blackberry, strawberry and raspberry. Most of these fruits have been specially bred by farmers from their wild relatives. The sweet, juicy apples that we eat today are very different from the wild 'crab' apples from which they were bred.

GAS A gas is quite different from a liquid or a solid. A solid has a definite shape and a definite size. A liquid does not have a definite shape but it does have a definite size. A gas has neither shape nor size. The smell of cabbage cooking can spread to every corner of the house.

The air we breathe is a mixture of gases. Most of it is oxygen and nitrogen. But oxygen and nitrogen are not always gases. If they are cooled they become liquids. And if they are cooled still more they become solids. The same is true of other gases.

Whether anything is a solid, a liquid, or a gas depends upon its temperature. A lump of iron is a solid. But if you heat iron it becomes a liquid. And if you heat it more, iron becomes a gas. Solids, liquids and gases are called the three states of matter.

GEMS For thousands of years rich and important people have worn ornaments of gold and beautiful coloured stones. These stones are called gems. Gems are mined from the ground. When they are first dug up they look like rough pebbles. Skilled men cut and polish the pebbles until they gleam and sparkle.

There are many different kinds of gems. Some of them are very difficult to find. This makes them very valuable. They are so valuable that they are often called precious stones. There are bright red rubies, deep blue sapphires, and brilliant green emeralds. The most precious of all gems are the clear, sparkling diamonds. The largest diamond ever found was called the Cullinan diamond. It was cut into two large stones and almost one hundred small stones. One is in the Queen's sceptre, the other is in her state crown.

Crown

As glaciers move, they smooth the ground beneath them. It is not the ice that smoothes the ground. It is the stones and boulders frozen in the ice which make a glacier like a giant piece of sandpaper.

Many, many years ago the weather was very cold and large parts of the world were buried beneath glaciers. The glaciers smoothed off hills and scraped soil from the land like giant bulldozers. This happened in the Great Ice Age.

GLASS The glass we use for windows, bottles, light bulbs and many other things is made mainly from sand. When sand is heated with other chemicals it turns into a syrupy liquid. When the liquid cools it becomes solid glass.

Glass is shaped in different ways. Sheets of glass for windows are made by pouring the syrupy liquid onto molten metal. Glass is lighter than metal so it floats on top. When the glass cools and becomes solid it can be lifted from the metal. Bottles are made by blowing blobs of melted glass into metal moulds.

GLIDER Not all aircraft need engines to fly. The glider stays aloft on air currents. Of course it must be launched into the air first. Flying in a glider is the nearest man has ever come to flying like a bird.

The giraffe's long legs and neck help it reach the juicy leaves of trees

GIRAFFE Even when it is first born a giraffe is as tall as a man. By the time it is fully grown it will be three times the size.

The giraffe lives on the great grassy plains of Africa. With its long legs and hooves it can quickly gallop away from its enemies. Because of its long neck and 18 inch tongue it also always has plenty of food. It can browse happily on the leaves at the tops of the trees which other animals cannot reach. It can also bend its neck down to the ground to eat grass and drink water. But it has to spread its legs far apart to do so.

GLACIER A glacier is a river of ice. It begins in high mountains where snow covers the ground all year round. As fresh snow falls, the snow beneath turns to ice. The ice grows thicker and thicker until it begins to move down the mountainside.

Glaciers are rivers of ice which flow down mountains. Sometimes glaciers reach the sea. Huge chunks of ice break off and float away as icebergs

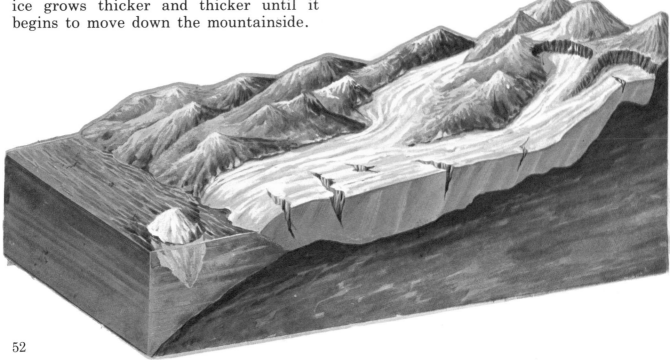

A glider is built in much the same way as a light aeroplane, only it is even lighter. It has the same kind of controls as an aeroplane. A glider is usually launched by being towed by a winch or a truck. The glider rises into the air just like a kite does when you pull it along the ground.

Over hilly country the glider soars upwards on rising air currents caused by the wind blowing against the hills. Over flat country the glider needs 'thermals' to keep it in the air. Thermals are air currents rising from warm ground or from cities. By moving from thermal to thermal, a glider pilot can travel long distances.

Goats are kept as domestic animals where the pasture is poor

GOAT Goats are sometimes called the 'poor man's cow'. Like cows and other cattle they chew the cud, but they do not need the rich grass that the fat farm cows eat. Goats live happily on poor, dry grass. They are kept by people in many parts of the world for their milk, meat, hair and skins.

Goats look rather like sheep but they have horns and tufts of hair on their chins which look like beards. Some goats are kept only for their hair. The soft fine hair of the Cashmere and Angora goats is very valuable.

Wild goats all live in the mountains. They have cloven hooves and special pads on their feet which help them to cling to the steep, rocky slopes.

GOLD One of the most precious metals of all is gold. It never corrodes and it is easy to shape because it is so soft. It can be made into all kinds of delicate and beautiful jewellery. Often other metals are mixed with gold to make it harder. Once gold was used to make coins. Now there are very few gold coins and most countries and banks store their gold in special strong vaults.

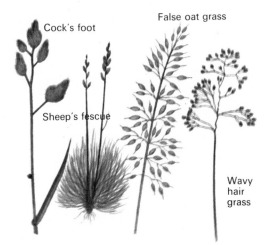

Cock's foot
False oat grass
Sheep's fescue
Wavy hair grass

Some of the many kinds of grasses

GRASS The plants of the grass family are very important. They provide men and animals with food. Rice, wheat, oats, barley, maize and sugar cane are all grasses. Grazing animals eat the leaves of the grasses. People mostly eat the seeds. Thousands and thousands of acres of land are used for growing crops to provide us with the rice and bread and sugar we need.

Most grasses are small, tough plants that can be cut, grazed and walked upon. Some are much bigger. Some bamboos grow up to 100 feet tall.

GRASSHOPPER It is easier to hear grasshoppers than to see them. They live close to the ground in the long grass. Their spiky bodies look rather like the blades of grass on which they cling. They make a very loud chirping noise by rubbing their back legs against their wings. Usually only the male sings. If you look closely at the grass when you hear the chirping noise you will probably catch sight of the grasshoppers as they jump with their long back legs. But remember, they jump very fast and only come out when the sun is shining.

A bush cricket is a kind of grasshopper

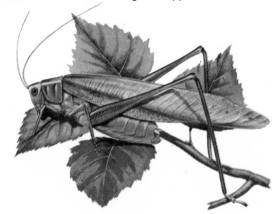

53

An ancient Greek painting showing women playing musical instruments

GREECE, ANCIENT The civilisation of Ancient Greece was more advanced than any that had gone before. Besides being fine builders and artists the Greeks were also the world's first great poets, playwrights, historians, and thinkers. They were also the first to study medicine and geometry.

Ancient Greece was not one united country. Each city or island formed its own *city-state*. Two of the greatest city-states were Sparta and Athens. The Greeks were the first to think of the idea of democracy. Ordinary citizens had a say in the running of the state.

The Greeks were skilled sailors. Wherever they travelled or traded they spread their knowledge and culture.

HEAT If you put a pan on a stove it soon gets hot. The pan does not look any different but something must have happened to it. If you could see the very tiny particles that make up the pan you would find that they were moving about faster than when the pan was cold.

The hotness or coldness of things is called their temperature. Instruments called thermometers measure temperature. In many thermometers the temperature at which water turns to ice is called 0 degrees and the temperature at which water boils is called 100 degrees. This is the Centigrade scale. The name comes from two words meanings 'one hundred steps'.

Heat can travel through a solid. It can travel through a liquid. It can even travel through space. Most of our heat travels through space from the Sun.

HEDGEHOG When it is frightened, the hedgehog rolls itself up into a tight ball. Its sharp spines stick out all round so that few animals will attack it.

Hedgehogs live in Europe, Asia and Africa. They are very peaceful creatures. They sleep during the day and hunt for food at night. They belong to a group of animals called insect-eaters but they eat slugs and worms and even bread and butter if it is left for them. In cold countries hedgehogs sleep for the whole of the winter. They collect dead leaves and pile them up into a nice, warm 'nest'.

Hedgehog

HELICOPTER The helicopter can do far more things than an aeroplane with wings. It can fly straight up or down. It can move forwards, backwards, or sideways. It can even hover like a hawk.

The helicopter has often been called a 'flying windmill' because of the long blades which whirl round above it. These blades are called the main rotor. The main rotor takes the place of both the wings and the propeller of other aeroplanes. There is another small rotor at the back. This stops the helicopter spinning round when the main rotor is turning.

Big helicopters have two main rotors. They spin in opposite directions

Helicopters are very useful because they do not need a runway to take off and land. They can fly from a flat roof in a city or from a jungle clearing. Helicopters are used to carry soldiers quickly from place to place, and to rescue people from the sea.

Dormouse

HIBERNATION Many animals spend the winter fast asleep. This sleep is called hibernation. Dormice hibernate. So do hedgehogs and bears and squirrels. Frogs and bees and butterflies also sleep through the winter. They sleep because in wintertime food is very scarce.

In the autumn the animals get ready to hibernate. They eat a great deal and they get very fat. Some of them, like squirrels, collect a store of food. They find a good place for a winter home. Holes in trees and in the ground make good winter homes. So do piles of leaves.

When the days get cold the animals fall asleep. Many of them do not wake up until spring. When they wake up they are very thin. During the winter their bodies have used up all the fat.

Hippopotamus

HIPPOPOTAMUS The name hippopotamus means 'river horse'. The hippopotamus is a huge, clumsy animal which lives in the swamps and rivers of Africa. It stays for hours in the water with only its eyes and nostrils showing. The hippopotamus has a huge mouth and big teeth. But it eats only plant food.

HORSE For thousands of years the horse has been one of the most useful animals to man in many parts of the world. Before locomotives and motor vehicles were invented, people travelled on horseback or in horse-drawn carriages. Horses pulled farmers' ploughs in the fields. They towed barges along canals. And they pulled heavy loads along the roads. Today locomotives and motor vehicles have replaced the horse. Few working horses are used. But many horses are kept for riding and racing.

Horse and foal

HOSPITALS When people are sick they sometimes need to go to a hospital. There they are cared for by doctors and nurses until they are well enough to go home.

The first hospitals were temples where people prayed to their gods to make them well again. In the middle ages there were hospitals in monasteries run by monks. Today there are many large hospitals to care for sick people. Modern hospitals are light and airy. And they are kept spotlessly clean.

Many highly skilled people are needed to run a modern hospital. Surgeons carry out operations. Doctors decide what treatment a sick person needs. Radiologists give patients x-rays. Pharmacologists make up medicines. And nurses look after the patients.

HOUSES The first men lived in caves. The caves protected them from the rain but they were not very comfortable. So men learnt how to build houses.

Houses can be built of many different things. People who live near forests build their houses of trees. People who live in rocky places build their houses of stone. In some places houses are built from bundles of reeds tied together. More reeds are used for the roofs. Many houses are built of dried mud. Bricks are made of dried clay.

People who live in very hot places build houses with thick walls. This makes them cool inside. They have very small windows so that the hot sunshine cannot get in. In colder countries houses have larger windows. The people who live in them like all the sunshine they can get.

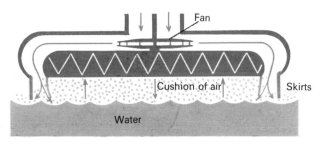

How a hovercraft works

HOVERCRAFT Boats are slower than cars, trains and aircraft. This is because they have to push their way through the water. Now there are special boats called hovercraft which are much faster. Hovercraft do not push their way through the water. They skim over the waves riding on a cushion of air. Air is pumped under the craft and kept there by flaps round the sides called skirts. Some of the air does escape, so more air must be pumped under the craft the whole time. The hovercraft is driven by propellers like an aeroplane.

Hovercraft can travel just as easily over the land as long as it is fairly flat. There may soon be trains which travel on a cushion of air instead of on wheels.

HURRICANE A hurricane is a violent storm which builds up over warm seas. It brings howling winds and lashing rain. The winds blow in a circle round a calm 'eye' in the middle of the storm. The winds may travel faster than an express train but the storm itself moves slowly across the sea.

If a hurricane crosses the coast it can cause a lot of damage. It can tear down houses and flood the land. In the past many people have been killed by hurricanes. Now weather forecasters are able to give people plenty of warning if a hurricane approaches. Weather satellites miles above the Earth can spot a hurricane as soon as it forms and radio information back to earth.

HYENA When animals like lions kill their prey they eat all the meat they can. Often there is some left. Then animals called scavengers come along to finish the left-over meat. Birds such as vultures are scavengers. So is the hyena.

The hyena looks rather like a large dog. It lives in Africa, India, and parts of Asia. Its strong jaws and teeth help it to crunch up large bones. It is famous for its strange howl, which sounds rather like a weird human laugh.

Hurricanes can cause great havoc

Some of the animals
that lived in the
Great Ice Age many
years ago

ICE AGE Long ago the climates of the world grew cold. As more and more snow fell, great ice sheets built up and moved across the land. Like giant bulldozers the ice sheets scraped the land clear of soil. They smoothed the tops of hills and the sides of valleys. They flattened forests and carried huge boulders hundreds of miles. This was the Great Ice Age when large parts of Europe, North America and Asia were buried beneath ice.

Many plants and animals died out during the Great Ice Age. Some animals fled south to warmer lands never to return. Other animals managed to survive in this endless winter. The mammoth and the woolly rhinoceros had thick coats to protect them from the bitter cold.

ICEBERG A glacier is a sheet of ice which moves slowly across the land. Sometimes glaciers reach the sea. When this happens, huge chunks of the glacier break off and float away. These floating pieces of ice are called icebergs. The word iceberg means 'mountain of ice'.

Some icebergs are miles wide and as tall as a skyscraper. But this is only the tip of the iceberg. There is eight or nine times as much ice under the water as there is above. This is why icebergs are a danger to ships. A ship may seem to have plenty of room to pass an iceberg, but it may hit the ice under the water.

One of the worst shipwrecks in this century was caused by an iceberg. The *Titanic*, the biggest liner at that time, struck an iceberg on her maiden voyage across the Atlantic in 1912 and sank. Today boats and aeroplanes patrol the seas watching for icebergs.

INCAS Hundreds of years ago people called Incas ruled over a huge empire in the mountains of South America. All the other people living there worked for the Incas. They farmed in the valleys. They built stone cities for the Incas. In the cities were huge temples where the Incas worshipped the sun. The cities were linked by winding roads. The Incas did not know how to make wheels. They did not have any horses. So messages were taken from one city to another by fast runners.

The Incas' rulers grew rich and powerful. They collected great treasures of gold. When explorers from Spain reached the Inca cities they saw the gold and riches. They wanted the treasure for themselves. They had guns and horses. It was easy for them to conquer the Incas. So the Spaniards became rulers of the huge Inca empire.

57

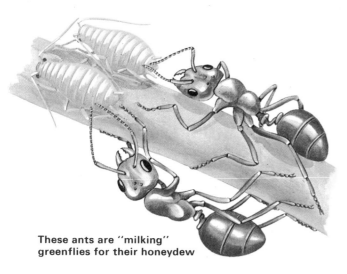

These ants are "milking" greenflies for their honeydew

INSECTS Butterflies, beetles and bees all belong to the great group of animals called insects. There are more kinds of insects than of all other animals added together. Insects have jointed bodies and three pairs of legs. Most of them have four wings but some, such as flies, have only two wings, and a few kinds are wingless. Attached to an insect's head are two feelers, or antennae, which the insect uses to smell and touch. An insect's body is covered with a hard outer casing called an exoskeleton.

Insects go through several stages as they grow. Some insects metamorphose or change through four different stages. The first stage is an egg. The second stage is a larva (a grub or caterpillar). The third stage is a pupa or chrysalis during which the insect changes into the fourth, adult stage. Butterflies grow like this. Other insects hatch from eggs and grow by shedding their skin a number of times. Gradually they look more and more like an adult. Dragonflies grow like this.

Many insects are useful to man. Bees help plants to make fruits and seeds by carrying pollen from flower to flower. Some insects eat plant pests. Others clear the ground of dead animals. But there are many insects which are harmful to man. Flies carry diseases. Other insects attack our crops and damage our homes.

IRON AND STEEL Iron was one of the first metals used by man. And it is still the most important metal of all because it is used to make steel. Bridges, skyscrapers, ships, cars and all kinds of machinery are made from steel.

Iron is found mixed with other chemicals in rocks. Rocks which contain a lot of iron are called iron ore. Iron ore is dug from the ground and put in a tall blast furnace with coke and limestone. It is called a blast furnace because blasts of hot air are blown through it to make the coke burn fiercer. It becomes so hot that the iron ore melts. Then chemical changes take place. The coke takes the oxygen from the iron ore. The limestone combines with impurities to make slag. Pure iron is left. It drips to the bottom of the furnace. The slag also falls to the bottom and floats on the iron. Every few hours the furnace is tapped. Tapping means taking out the pure iron and the slag. The iron comes out of one opening, the slag out of another. A blast furnace goes on working day and night.

Most of the iron made in blast furnaces goes to other furnaces to be made into steel. Steel is iron with other chemicals added to it, particularly carbon. There are many different steels. Some are very hard. They are used for cutting tools. Some will not rust. These are called stainless steels.

When the molten steel leaves the furnace it is poured into moulds called ingots. There it cools and hardens. Then it is sent to rolling mills to be shaped.

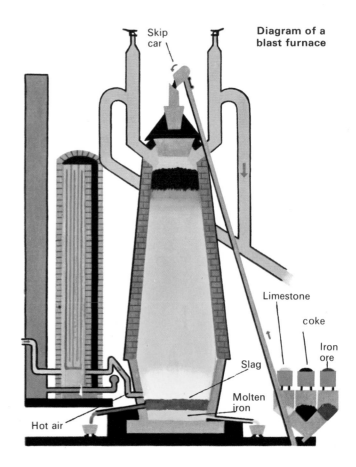

Diagram of a blast furnace

Skip car

Limestone

coke

Iron ore

Slag

Molten iron

Hot air

Brightly coloured plants and animals
live in the jungle tree-tops

JELLYFISH The jellyfish is a sea animal with a transparent body. It floats in the water and catches food with its stinging tentacles. The common jellyfish has a dome-shaped body with tentacles hanging beneath. It moves by squirting jets of water from its body. The Portuguese-man-o'-war is a large jellyfish. It is really lots of small jellyfish hanging beneath a gas-filled bag. The Portugese-man-o'-war has a nasty sting which can hurt bathers.

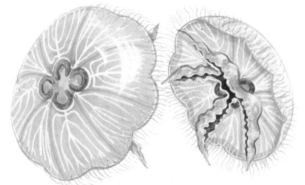

The common jellyfish showing its stinging tentacles

JUNGLE In some parts of the world the weather is always hot and it rains nearly every day. Huge forests grow in these places. Sometimes they are called jungles. But a better name is rain forests. Rain forests seem damp and gloomy places when you walk through them. The trees grow so close together that their leaves blot out the sunlight. The ground is mostly bare soil. But if you look down on a rain forest there are many bright colours. Huge butterflies flit over the trees. Chattering monkeys and brightly coloured birds live in the tree tops. And beautiful orchids grow in the topmost branches.

Because there is so much rain there are many rivers in the rain forests. They are used instead of roads by people to travel from place to place. But few people live in the rain forests. There are some parts which are still unexplored.

KANGAROO The kangaroo is the largest of the marsupials. A marsupial is a mammal which carries its young in a pouch. A fully-grown red kangaroo may be taller than a man. Kangaroos live only in Australia. They feed mainly on grass. Kangaroos travel around in groups called mobs. A mob is led by an old male called a boomer.

The big hind legs of a kangaroo are very powerful. A kangaroo can jump along faster than a man can run. It uses its big tail to balance itself. The front legs are much smaller. A kangaroo rests on all four legs only when it is eating.

The kangaroo lives in Australia. It carries its young in a pouch. Kangeroos travel in groups called mobs

The koala carries its young in a pouch as it climbs through the branches of eucalyptus trees. Eucalyptus leaves are the only food koalas eat

KOALA The koala is a small, furry Australian animal which looks very much like a teddy bear. But the koala is not a bear. It is a marsupial. A marsupial is a mammal which rears its young in a pouch on the mother's body.

The koala lives in trees, holding tightly to branches with its strong claws. Koalas feed only on the leaves of eucalyptus trees.

LAKES A lake is an area of water which is completely surrounded by land. Some lakes are so big they are called seas. The Caspian Sea in Asia is the largest lake in the world. The water of the Caspian is salty. The largest freshwater lake is Lake Superior in North America. Lake Superior is one of the Great Lakes. There are five in all.

Many lakes were made during the Great Ice Age thousands of years ago when many lands were buried beneath ice. The ice scraped out hollows in the land. When the ice melted the hollows filled with water. Some large lakes are man-made. They form when dams are built across rivers.

LEAF One of the most important differences between plants and animals is that plants can make their own food while animals cannot. A plant's food is made in its leaves. Each leaf is a tiny food factory.

The green colour of a leaf comes from a marvellous pigment called chlorophyll. The chlorophyll uses the energy of sunlight to make sugars from water and a gas called carbon dioxide. The water is carried into the leaf by small veins. The carbon dioxide comes from the air. It enters the leaf through tiny holes called stomata.

This wonderful food-making process is called photosynthesis. It can only take place in sunlight. That is why few plants grow well in very shady places.

There are many different shapes of leaves and they are arranged on the stem in different ways. It is possible to tell most plants from their leaves.

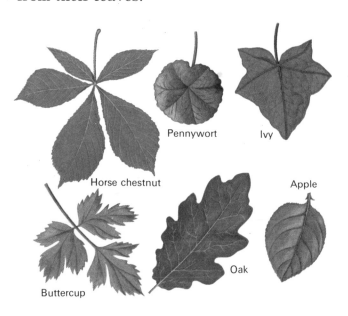

Pennywort

Ivy

Horse chestnut

Apple

Buttercup

Oak

LEOPARD The leopard is one of the biggest members of the cat family. Only lions and tigers are larger. Leopards live in Africa and Asia. Most are brown with black spots, but some leopards are black. These are called panthers. Leopards climb trees well and are fierce hunters. A close relative of the leopard lives in the mountains of Asia. It is called the snow leopard or ounce. The jaguar is an American cousin of the leopard.

A jaguar and its cub

LICHENS The grey, crusty covering you often see on rocks and tree trunks is made of tiny plants called lichens. Lichens grow in places where other plants would find it impossible to live.

A lichen is really two plants in one. One part of it is a fungus. The other part is a tiny green plant called an alga. The fungus cannot make its own food. Instead, it takes in water and minerals for the alga. The alga uses the water and sunlight to make food for both itself and the fungus.

Lichens growing on a rock

LIGHT Without light we could not see anything. We see things because light comes from them to our eyes. We see the Sun, the stars and the flames of a fire because they make their own light. But most of the things we see do not make their own light. They reflect light to our eyes. During the day they reflect the light of the Sun. In the dark we use torches and electric lamps to make light so that we can see things.

Most of our light comes from the Sun. Even at night there is a little light from the Sun. We call it moonlight because it seems to come from the Moon. But the Moon does not make its own light. It reflects the light of the Sun.

Light travels very fast. The Sun is many millions of miles from the Earth. But rays of light take only a few minutes to reach us.

Light always travels in straight lines. That is why we cannot see round corners. And that is why we cannot see places which are far away. The light reflected from them will not bend round the curve of the Earth to our eyes.

Light is important because it lets us see. It is even more important for plants. They need sunlight to make their food. Without sunlight there could be no plants. And without plants there could be no animals.

LIGHTNING A flash of lightning is a huge spark of electricity. It may go from one cloud to another or it may jump from a cloud to the ground in a jagged streak. The spark heats the air and makes it expand with a rumbling bang. We call this noise thunder. Thunder is heard some seconds after a flash of lightning because sound travels much slower than light.

The male lion has
a long, shaggy mane

match its surroundings. The frilled lizard raises a frill round its neck to frighten away its enemies.

LLAMA The llama is a relative of the camel. But it is smaller and has no hump on its back. Llamas live in the mountains of South America. They are used to carry goods over the narrow mountain roads. Llamas are very irritable animals. They spit when they are angry.

LION The lion is often called 'king of the beasts'. It is certainly one of the strongest and fiercest of wild animals. When a lion is hungry few animals are safe. The lion is also sometimes called 'the lord of the jungle'. But lions do not live in jungles. They live on the grassy plains of Africa and India in family groups called prides.

A male lion is one of the biggest members of the cat family. It has a long mane on its shoulders. A female lion, or lioness, is smaller and has no mane. The lioness does most of the hunting for the pride. The male lions and the cubs spend most of their time basking in the sun.

The Indians of South America use the llama's long hair to make cloth and its hide to make sandals

LIZARDS There are many different kinds of lizards living in the warmer parts of the world. Most are fairly small creatures which hide from the sun during the day under rocks. They come out at night to hunt for food. A few lizards grow quite large. Largest of all is the Komodo dragon which is as big as an alligator.

All lizards have scaly skins and most lay eggs. Lizards eat insects and small animals. The chameleon catches insects by shooting out its long tongue. Only two lizards have a poisonous bite. One is the gila monster which lives in the deserts of North America.

Most lizards scuttle over the ground on four stumpy legs. But some can run on their hind legs. Some can glide from tree to tree by stretching out loose folds of skin like sails. And one kind of lizard has no legs at all. Legless lizards wriggle over the ground like snakes. They are called slow worms.

Lizards have strange ways of escaping their enemies. Many lizards can shed their tail. The chameleon changes colour to

LOCUST The locust is an insect belonging to the grasshopper family. It is one of the worst plant pests in northern Africa and south-west Asia. Locust live in dry lands. Sometimes they band together in huge swarms which make the sky quite dark. Wherever the swarm settles the locusts eat every green leaf and blade of grass in sight, ruining crops and pastures. Aircraft are now used to destroy them by spraying the swarms with poison.

Australian frilled lizard

MAGNET Long ago, the Greeks found a kind of rock which would pull to it, or attract, pieces of iron. The rock was a natural magnet. The word 'magnet' comes from the name of the place where the rock was first found. It was called Magnesia.

The ends of a magnet are called poles. One end is a north pole. The other end is a south pole. When the north pole of a magnet

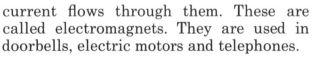

The thick coat of the woolly mammoth helped it to survive the cold of the Great Ice Age

is put near the south pole of another magnet the two poles attract each other. But when the north poles or south poles of two magnets are put together they repel each other. To repel means to push away.

Long after magnets had been discovered, it was found that they could be used to find the direction of North. If a magnet is allowed to swing freely it will come to rest

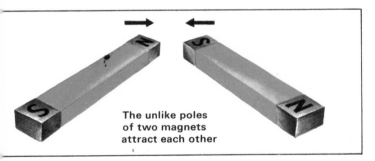

The unlike poles of two magnets attract each other

with one end pointing north. A pocket compass is simply a magnetic needle which can swing round on a pin.

Natural magnets are called permanent magnets because they keep their magnetism. Permanent magnets can also be made from iron and steel. There are other magnets which do not keep their magnetism. They become magnets only when an electric current flows through them. These are called electromagnets. They are used in doorbells, electric motors and telephones.

MAMMOTH Long ago the climates of the world grew cold and many lands were covered by ice. This was the Great Ice Age. Many animals died out. Others fled to warmer lands. But some animals managed to survive in the snow and ice. They were protected from the bitter cold by a thick, shaggy coat. The largest of these animals was the mammoth. The mammoth was related to the elephants of today. It had huge tusks and a long trunk.

There are no mammoths alive today. They were all killed by cavemen for food. But we know exactly what they looked like. Mammoths have been found preserved in ice in cold lands.

MAPS A map is a drawing which shows how cities, roads, railways, mountains, rivers and many other things are arranged on the surface of the Earth. Many maps are drawings of a very small part of the world. Other maps show the whole world.

No one map can show everything. Some maps show cities, roads and railways. Some show mountains, plains, rivers and lakes. There are many other special maps. They may show how much rain falls in different parts of the world, how hot it is, or how many people live in different places. Many different kinds of maps are found in books called atlases.

MEDICINE When you have a cough you sometimes swallow some cough mixture to make it better. Cough mixture is a kind of medicine. There are many different kinds of medicine to make different illnesses better. Some of them come in bottles like the cough mixture. Others are made into little tablets. The ointments which help cuts and sore places to heal are medicines too.

Medicines are bought in chemists' shops. Some medicines are very strong. You can only buy them if you take the chemist a note from a doctor. It is dangerous to take more medicine than the doctor tells you. And it can be dangerous to take the wrong medicine. Most people keep medicines in a special place so that they cannot be taken by mistake.

METALS Everything in the world is made out of simple substances called elements. There are about one hundred different elements and more than half of them are metals. Some of the best known metals are iron, copper, aluminium, silver, gold, and lead. But there are many other important metals with strange names such as hafnium, molybdenum, osmium, yttrium and zirconium.

Most metals are hard, shiny and silvery in colour. But a few metals, such as copper and gold, are coloured. A few are soft enough to be cut with a knife. And one metal is a liquid. It is called mercury.

Many of the metals we use are mixtures. They are called alloys. Brass, bronze and steel are three well known alloys. Brass is a mixture of copper and zinc. Bronze is a

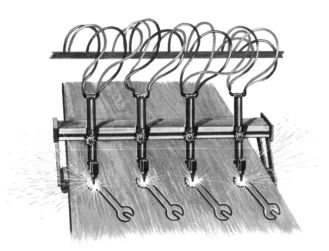

Special gas torches are used to "cut" metal tools

mixture of copper and tin. Steel is a mixture of iron and carbon. Carbon is not a metal. Other metals are often added to steel to make it very hard or stainless.

Gold and silver are sometimes found as metals in the ground. Most other metals are never found free. They are always combined with other elements in rocks. Rocks which contain a lot of metal are called ores.

Ores are dug from the ground and the metal is taken from them. This is often done by heating the ore in a furnace. Special substances are added which combine with the other elements in the ore. They form a layer of slag which floats on the pure metal.

Metals are shaped in many ways. Molten metal can be poured into a mould. The metal cools and becomes solid in the same shape as the mould. This is called casting. Metal can also be pounded or squeezed into shape by powerful hammers and presses. Steel sheets and girders are made by passing the metal between powerful rollers. Wire is made by pulling metal through a small hole.

METEOR On its journey round the Sun the Earth collides with many pieces of rock called meteors. As these rocks plunge through the air, friction makes them glow white-hot. We call them 'shooting stars'. Meteors usually burn up in the air. Those which do reach the ground are called meteorites. The biggest meteorite to hit the Earth landed in Arizona in prehistoric times. It made a crater 600 feet deep and almost a mile across.

MICROSCOPE There are countless living things which are too small to be seen with our eyes. We know about them through microscopes. A microscope is like a very powerful magnifying glass. It has glass lenses which make tiny objects look thousands of times bigger than they really are.

The most powerful microscopes of all do not use light and glass lenses to magnify. Instead they shoot a stream of very tiny particles called electrons past an object. The electrons make a greatly magnified picture of the object on a special screen. With an electron microscope it is possible to 'see' things which are less than one millionth of an inch across.

Microscopes have helped doctors to find the cause of many diseases. They have also helped scientists to make many discoveries.

Globigerina, a microscopic animal

Amoeba

Coscinodiscus, a microscopic plant.

Paramecium is only 1/100 inch long.

A microscope has a series of lenses which make objects appear hundreds of times larger than they really are

MICROSCOPIC LIFE Some plants and animals are so small that you can only see them with the aid of a microscope. The smallest creatures have only one cell. In the cell there is a dark spot which is its nucleus, or 'brain'.

The amoeba is a single-celled animal which looks like a blob of jelly. It feeds on tiny plants which it draws into the cell with small 'fingers'. Even smaller than the single-celled animals are bacteria. Two thousand of the very biggest bacteria laid end to end would hardly make an inch. Viruses are the smallest of all living things. They cause many diseases.

The algae are very simple plants and many of them are microscopic. They live mostly in the water and some of them can move about like animals. They have *flagella* that drive them through the water like oars. The microscopic algae in the sea are very important. They are the basic food of many sea animals, including even the largest whale.

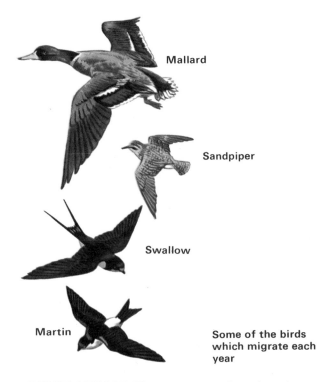

Mallard

Sandpiper

Swallow

Martin

Some of the birds which migrate each year

MIGRATION Every year the Arctic tern flies about 22 thousand miles from one end of the world to the other and back again. It flies away from the freezing winter cold in the Arctic to the summer warmth of the Antarctic. When the winter comes to the Antarctic it flies back to the Arctic. Not many animals make journeys as long as that but many others do move from place to place at certain times of the year. These movements are called migrations. The caribou of the Arctic and the mountain goats and sheep move down to the forests as the weather gets cold in the winter. Painted Lady butterflies fly all the way from Iceland to Africa to find warmer weather.

Some animals make long journeys to breed. Frogs, toads, and newts spend most of their time on land. In spring they must return to the water to lay their eggs. The European eel swims all the way from the rivers of Europe to the Sargasso sea to lay its eggs and the salmon makes a long, hard journey up river from the sea to the place where it was born.

Nobody is quite sure how the animals find their way from place to place. Birds often return to exactly the same nesting place after flying half way round the world. Some scientists think that they are guided by the stars.

MILK All mammals produce milk in their bodies to feed their young. Milk is a very important food. It contains more goodness than any other. We get our milk from cows, sheep, goats and camels. We drink it and use it to make butter, cream, cheese and many other things.

MINERALS Some rocks are speckled. If you look closely at them you will see that they are made up of lots of little pieces. Some may be jet black. Some may be white and shiny. Some may be brightly coloured. These little pieces are minerals. All rocks are made of minerals. Some rocks are made of just one mineral. Other rocks have lots of different minerals in them. There are thousands of different minerals in the world. Some are very important to us. Metals and jewels come from minerals. Minerals which are mined for the metals they contain are called ores.

Most minerals are found as crystals in rocks. Some of the crystals have beautiful shapes and colours. The most common mineral is quartz. Nearly every grain of sand is a tiny piece of quartz. But some quartz crystals are very beautiful. Many precious stones are coloured quartz.

Minerals have many beautiful shapes and colours

Many minerals are mined deep underground

MINING The rocks of the Earth are a treasure chest of minerals. They contain all of the coal, oil and metals we use. Taking these minerals from the ground is called mining.

Some mines are simply great holes in the ground. The minerals are scooped up by great shovels and dumped in trucks. This is called open-cast mining.

Most minerals are found deep under the ground. A wide shaft is dug down to the mineral-bearing rocks. Then tunnels are dug outwards from the bottom of the shaft. The minerals are either cut out by powerful machines or loosened by blasting with explosives. A lot of coal and metals are mined in this way. Some of the mines are two miles deep and some have tunnels running out beneath the sea bed.

Machines do most of the work that miners used to do by hand. But working deep underground is still difficult and dangerous. Great care must be taken to avoid accidents. Tunnels are supported by strong beams to prevent them collapsing and fresh air is pumped through the tunnels all the time.

MIRAGE People travelling in the desert have sometimes seen a pool of water surrounded by trees a short distance away. But when they have rushed towards it, the pool has disappeared. These people have seen a mirage. It was not their imagination. The pool was real enough. But it was probably many miles away. A mirage is a trick of the light which makes objects appear in a different place from where they really are. It is caused by light passing through layers of cold and hot air. The layers bend the rays of light.

Mirages are not only seen in deserts. They are sometimes seen at sea. A ship which is over the horizon may occasionally appear in the sky.

MIRROR A mirror is a smooth surface which sends back rays of light. Mirrors are usually made of highly polished glass which has a thin layer of silver on the back. They can also be made of polished metal. When you look in the mirror you see your *reflection*. All reflections are turned round. You can see this most clearly if you hold up a printed page to the mirror. The letters go the wrong way and you have to read them from right to left.

Mirages are sometimes seen in deserts

Mole

MOLE The mole is a small mammal with soft fur that lives almost entirely underground. Moles are tireless diggers. They use their strong, clawed front feet to loosen the earth and shovel it back with their hind feet. They search for food as they burrow, eating earthworms and grubs. Moles are nearly blind but they have very sharp hearing.

MONEY When people first began to trade they used to exchange or 'swop' goods. So many pots or measures of wheat might be bartered for a sheep, and so on. But this way of doing business was very clumsy, so money was invented.

Coins were often made of gold or silver. But they can be made of anything—so long as everyone agrees on how much they are worth. Today notes are used as well as coins. A £20 pound note is itself worth little. What it will buy is worth a lot.

Each country has its own money—American dollars, French francs, and German marks, for example. When you travel, you have to change your money into that of the country you are visiting. This is done at an agreed rate of exchange. You get so many francs or dollars for your pound, which is rather like the old barter system.

MONKEYS Many people think that all monkeys can grip branches and swing by their tails, but it is not true. Only the

A family of baboons

monkeys that live in America can do that. They are called New World monkeys and their tails are called 'prehensile' tails. Spider monkeys often hang from the branches of the trees so that they can scoop up water and even fishes with their hands.

Lots of monkeys live in the hot forests of Africa and Asia. They are Old World monkeys. Many of them live on the ground. Baboons live in big family groups. One big male leads them and the other males protect the females and babies.

Only one side of the Moon is ever seen from the Earth

MOON The Moon is the Earth's nearest neighbour. It goes round the Earth, just as the Earth goes round the Sun. The Moon takes about 27 days to orbit (circle) the Earth. During that time it spins round once, so it always keeps the same side facing the Earth. Until men sent spacecraft there, nobody had ever seen the far side of the Moon.

The Moon is about one quarter the size of the Earth in *diameter*—that is, from one side to the other. It has no air and no water, and therefore people, animals, and plants cannot live naturally there. Men who visit the Moon have to take their own air and water with them. The surface of the Moon is dry and rocky, with a great deal of dust. The Moon does not send out light like the Sun. Moonlight is the light of the Sun reflected as if by a giant mirror.

The first man to land on the Moon, Neil Armstrong, did so on July 20, 1969. Other astronauts have since explored parts of the Moon.

The female mosquito has a long tube which she uses to pierce the skin of animals and suck up a little of their blood

MOSQUITO The mosquito is a fly that carries the disease of malaria. The female mosquito lives on the blood of other animals, including people. She pierces the skin with a long tube from her mouth and sucks up the blood. As she does so she pours juice in the wound to stop the blood going hard. This is when the disease is passed on.

The name malaria is an Italian word meaning 'bad air'. People often fell ill with the disease when they travelled through the marshes of Italy. They thought it was the hot, steamy 'bad air' that was making them ill. Really it was the mosquitoes that lived in the swamps.

MOUNTAINS About one fifth of all the world's land is covered by mountains. A mountain rises at least 2,000 feet above the land around it. High ground lower than 2,000 feet is known as a *hill*. The world's highest mountains are the Himalayas, in Asia, lying between India and China. Other important mountain regions are the Alps, in Europe; the Rockies, in North America; and the Andes, in South America. There are only a few mountains in Africa and Australia. But there are many mountains under the great oceans.

Mountains are made by movements of the *crust*, or outer layer, of the Earth. Most of these movements take millions of years. Some mountains are formed by *volcanoes*, which shoot jets of red-hot rock called lava out of the ground. Some islands in the Pacific Ocean have been formed in this way. They are really the tips of underwater mountains that project above the surface of the sea.

MUSHROOMS AND TOADSTOOLS If you go out into a field early in the morning you may see mushrooms growing in the grass. They look like little umbrellas. A mushroom is a kind of fungus. Fungi are plants that cannot make food like green plants.

Mushrooms and toadstools do not have seeds. They grow from spores. Many mushrooms, like the meadow mushroom, are good to eat but some are poisonous toadstools. Only experts can tell which ones are poisonous, so it is best never to pick them. The death cap toadstool is so poisonous that it can kill a man. Even the pretty red and white fly agaric toadstool can make you very, very ill.

Morels, puff-balls, chanterelles and truffles can all be eaten. In France, pigs are used to hunt for truffles because they grow underground and people cannot smell where they are. When they find them, the pigs are rewarded with acorns which they like almost as much as truffles.

Fly agaric toadstool   Meadow mushroom

Guitar

Violin

Oboe

Clarinet

French horn

Trumpet

Triangle

Accordian

Bagpipes

Harp

MUSIC When people are happy they often sing. Singing is a kind of music. Music is made up of pleasant sounds called notes. There are high notes and low notes. These notes can be sounded for a long time or for a short time. We can make patterns of long and short notes called rhythms. We can arrange high and low notes and long and short notes into tunes.

We can make music by singing and whistling. And we can make it with musical instruments. If you blow down a hollow pipe you can make it sound a musical note. Men have made hollow pipes of many different shapes and sizes. They are called wind instruments. The recorder and the flute are wind instruments made of wood. The trumpet is a wind instrument made of brass.

Many instruments are made from strings of metal or gut stretched tight across wooden boxes. If you move the strings, for instance by plucking them, they sound notes. Short strings give high notes. Long strings give low notes. The carefully shaped wooden boxes make the notes sound louder. These are called stringed instruments. The guitar is a stringed instrument. So is the violin.

Many things give out pleasant sounds when they are hit. Instruments which are hit are called percussion instruments. Drums and triangles are both percussion instruments.

Very often groups of people with different instruments play together. The tune each instrument plays is different. But the tunes have been written so that they sound nice together. These groups are called orchestras.

NESTS Many animals build homes in which to live and raise their young. Birds are among the cleverest home builders. Many birds build simple nests of leaves and twigs. Others build strange nests. The weaver bird makes its nest by sewing two leaves together with the stem of a plant. The mistletoe bird builds a snow-white nest at the top of a tree. It is made from cobwebs and the feathery 'down' from seeds. The oven bird makes its nest from mud. When the mud dries in the sun it is as hard as a brick house.

The weaver bird makes its nest by sewing together two leaves

NEWSPAPERS People who work on newspapers are sometimes called the Press. The person in charge of a newspaper is the editor. The editor decides what will be printed. Under the editor comes the news editor who arranges the general news. The sports editor looks after the sports pages.

The news is sent in by reporters. Their reports are checked and prepared for printing by sub-editors. Most big newspapers also have correspondents who live in foreign countries. They send back reports. Newspapers may also buy news from news agencies.

The features editor looks after special articles on any topic that is in the news. There are also those who deal with pictures, cartoons, or the children's page.

The advertising department is also very important. Without advertisements newspapers would cost much more than they do. The money people pay to put in an advertisement helps to pay for the newspaper.

Warty newt

Smooth newt

NEWTS The newts are long-tailed cousins of the frogs and toads. Like them, newts can breathe through their skins. They live mostly in the water although they have short legs for moving on land. They often spend the summer on land and in winter they hibernate because they are cold-blooded. They would freeze if they did not keep warm.

NEW ZEALAND New Zealand is an island country in the South Pacific Ocean. It consists of two big islands, North Island and South Island, and a few small islands. It is almost as big as the British Isles. The country has a number of low mountains, and many forests. In North Island is an area where there are many springs of hot water or boiling mud. The weather is generally mild and pleasant. Most of the people live in North Island. Nearly all of them are descended from British or Irish people who settled there. There are also some Maoris, dark skinned people who were the first persons to live there. New Zealand has many sheep, and produces a great deal of wool and meat. Canterbury lamb comes from an area of New Zealand known as Canterbury.

New Zealand shares Britain's Queen Elizabeth II as its ruler. It is a member of the Commonwealth, a group of countries founded by Britain.

Maoris were the first people to live in New Zealand

Pictures of New Zealand

Mount Cook is New Zealand's highest mountain

Butter-making machine

Space launch

Timber

Wheat fields

Oil wells

Highways

Baseball

Skyscrapers

NORTH AMERICA North America is the world's third largest *continent* (area of land). It is more than twice the size of Europe. But three times as many people live in Europe as in North America. The northern part of the continent lies north of the Arctic Circle, and is always very cold. The southern part is always warm.

Most of North America is made up of two countries, Canada and the United States. The rest consists of Mexico and the little countries of Central America. North America is linked to South America by a narrow strip of land called the Isthmus of Panama. The Panama Canal runs through this strip of land so that ships can move between the Atlantic and Pacific oceans.

A great deal of the northern part of North America is low-lying, rocky land, with many icy lakes and rivers, and forests. Further south in the east is a long range of mountains, the Appalachians. In the west are the high, rugged Rocky Mountains. A great deal of the centre is covered by wide, rolling plains, where buffalo used to roam. Now cattle graze there, and wheat and maize (corn) are grown. There are many big rivers. The St. Lawrence River runs east-west between Canada and the United States. Large ships sail up it to the Great Lakes, five huge lakes named Superior, Michigan, Huron, Erie, and Ontario. The Niagara Falls lies between lakes Erie and Ontario. Further south the mighty Mississippi River runs southwards to the Gulf of Mexico.

There are many wild animals in North America, though hunters have killed a great many of them. They include bears, beavers, elk, moose, deer, porcupines, and eagles. In the south are alligators, snakes, and wild turkeys.

The land is rich in metals such as copper, gold, iron, lead, silver and nickel, and other minerals such as petroleum and natural gas.

Until the 1500s North America was an empty land with only a few American Indians living in it. Since then millions of Europeans have gone there and also Negroes from Africa. Now North America is one of the most important parts of the world.

Pictures of North America

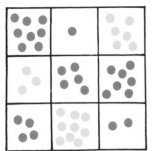

These are magic squares. The sum of every row of numbers is the same

NUMBERS When we count we use numbers. We write these down with ten symbols: 1, 2, 3, 4, 5, 6, 7, 8, 9, and 0. These symbols were thought up by the Arabs. We call them Arabic numerals.

Different people all over the world have thought up different systems of numbers. Many of them were written with simple up and down strokes. The Roman system of numbers was used for hundreds of years. 1, 2, and 3 were written I, II, and III. But IIII for 4 was starting to get muddling. As 5 was V, the Romans usually used IV for 4. This meant one less than five. The symbol for 10 was X. So 12 was XII—two more than ten.

Most systems count in tens. Perhaps this is because we have ten fingers, and people who are bad at counting can use their fingers to help them.

NYLON Once shirts, socks, stockings and dresses were made of cotton or silk or wool. Now they are made from artificial materials as well. Nylon is the most important artificial fibre. It was first made by an American chemist called Wallace Carothers. It is made completely from chemicals. A mixture of two chemicals, taken from coal tar, petrol or natural gas, is heated in a 'cooker' and the liquid is forced through tiny holes to make long, thin fibres. The fibres are very strong. When made into fabric, nylon does not wear out or rot. It needs no ironing and it drips dry.

OASIS It is very hard for people to live in deserts. Most of desert lands are covered with sand and rocks. There is no water for them to drink. There is no grass for their animals to eat. But scattered over the desert are oases. Here the water far below the surface of the desert has risen up in springs. Grass can grow round the oasis. So can palm trees. The desert people can get food and water. Their animals can graze. And the trees give them shade from the burning sun.

An oasis is a welcome sight to travellers in the desert

An octopus has eight long tentacles

OCEANS Nearly three-quarters of the Earth's surface is covered by water. We call the largest areas of water oceans. Smaller areas of water near land are called *seas*, *gulfs*, or *bays*. But we also use the word *sea* to describe all the oceans and seas together. There are three big oceans. The largest is the Pacific, between Asia and America. Then comes the Atlantic, between America on one side and Europe and Africa on the other. The third is the Indian Ocean, which lies south of India, between Africa and Australia. North of Europe, Asia, and America lies a fourth ocean, the Arctic Ocean. Most of this ocean is always covered with ice. Some people describe the southernmost parts of the Pacific, Atlantic, and Indian oceans as a fifth ocean, the Antarctic Ocean.

OCTOPUS With its eight long tentacles, big head and rows of suckers, the octopus looks very frightening. But it is not a dangerous animal. Even the biggest octopus, which is about 30 feet across, is quite peaceful.

The floor of the oceans has plains, valleys and mountains greater than any on the land

Octopuses move by pulling themselves along with their suckers or by shooting out a jet of water from a special 'siphon'. This propels the octopus backwards through the water.

The octopus is usually well hidden from its enemies because its skin can change colour to match its background. But when it is very frightened it has a good way of escaping. It squirts out an inky liquid which clouds the water while the octopus makes its getaway.

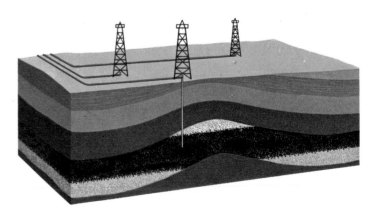

Oil is found trapped in rocks beneath the ground

OIL Oil, sometimes called petroleum, is a dark, greasy liquid that is found deep under the ground. In some places oil is found in the ground that lies under the sea. Men drill holes into the Earth, called oilwells, to extract the oil. Then they refine (purify) the oil to make many products that are useful to us. The most important are the fuels, such as petrol (gasoline), diesel oil, and kerosene or paraffin, which power motor-cars, ships,

railway locomotives, and aeroplanes. Another product is the *lubricating oil* you put on machinery to make it run smoothly. We also make many other things from oil, including paint, detergents for washing dishes and clothes, and explosives.

OLYMPIC GAMES Every four years athletes from all over the world meet to take part in competitions. These competitions are called the Olympic Games. They get their name from games which were held hundreds of years ago in ancient Greece.

Many different sports take place during the Olympic Games. There are swimming and running races. There are gymnastic competitions. There are hockey matches and shooting competitions. The people who enter these competitions cannot be paid. They are called amateurs. The winners of the competitions are given gold medals. An Olympic gold medal is the highest prize a sportsman can get.

ORANGES AND LEMONS Citrus trees are grown in many warm countries. They have beautiful flowers with a lovely smell. Oranges, lemons, grapefruits, tangerines and limes are all citrus fruits.

The fruits contain a sharp acid. You can taste it in lemons. It is called citric acid. Oranges have more sugar in them so you cannot taste the sourness. Tangerines are small orange-like fruits. Limes look like green lemons and are grown for their juice rather than the fruit itself. On long voyages, sailing ships carried limes to prevent the

crew getting scurvy a disease caused by lack of vitamin C. All citrus fruits contain vitamin C.

An ostrich cannot fly, but it can run very fast

OSTRICH The fully grown ostrich is about eight feet tall. It is the largest living bird but it cannot fly. It lives on the plains of Africa. Unlike almost all other birds it has only two toes, like the hooves of the antelopes that live by its side. It is a very shy creature but it does not really bury its head in the sand. When it is frightened it usually runs for its life.

There are not many ostriches left alive now. They have been hunted for their feathers and their great eggs have been stolen. Once they lived all over Africa but most of them are now found in National Parks.

Otters have smooth, soft fur

OTTER The otter is a furry animal that lives in or near water. Its fur is soft, warm and valuable. Because of this, it has been hunted and trapped until now there are few left alive.

Otters are very good swimmers. They use their strong tails as rudders. River otters live in burrows in the river bank and catch fish, frogs, snails and other creatures for food. Sea otters eat crabs, sea-urchins and shellfish, but, strangely, they do not eat fish.

OWLS People are sometimes called as wise as owls. Owls certainly look very wise. They have large eyes and the feathers grow round them so that they look as if they were wearing spectacles.

Owls are night birds. Their sharp eyes can see little night animals like rats and mice. They fly so silently that their prey cannot hear them. Then they pounce down on them and carry them off in their powerful claws. On bright nights their prey can sometimes see an owl's shadow moving across the ground. Then they can hide.

Owls make a hooting noise. It is often written down as 'too wit, too woo'. Some owls make a harsh squawk. They are called screech owls.

Owl

OYSTER Most precious gems come from rocks or mines. The pearl is the only one made by a living creature. The oyster is a mollusc which is valued for its taste. It is even more highly prized for the pearls it makes.

The oyster has two shells to protect its soft body. Sometimes a grain of sand gets inside the shells and makes the little animal uncomfortable. So the oyster covers the sand with the smooth, shiny stuff that lines its shell. This stops it hurting and also makes a pearl. That is why the lining of an oyster shell is called mother-of-pearl.

Pearls are found in oysters

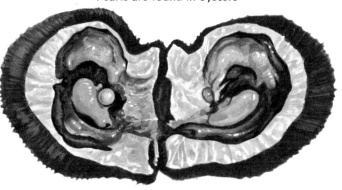

OXYGEN All living things need the gas oxygen to stay alive. About one-fifth of the air is oxygen. People and other animals take in oxygen when they breathe. The body needs the oxygen to 'burn' its food and produce energy. We breathe out the gas carbon dioxide. Plants breathe in oxygen, too, but during the day they also use large amounts of carbon dioxide and give off oxygen.

Nothing can burn without oxygen. It is often used in industry in gas torches for cutting and welding metals. It is also used to drive rockets into space.

PAINTING No one knows why men began to paint. Perhaps they believed that by painting likenesses of animals or gods they would get special powers. By drawing pictures of animals being hunted, men may have thought that they would become fine hunters.

Painting was used to decorate the vases and pots of ancient Greeks and Egyptians. Wall-paintings adorned the houses of many ancient peoples. These frescoes were painted on wet plaster.

Cave painting

The Christian Church used paintings to tell stories from the Bible. Many religious 'masterpieces' were painted in Italy. Giotto, Botticelli, and Michelangelo are just some of these great artists.

Italian ideas about painting spread to northern Europe. The great Flemish artists Breughel and Rubens painted portraits and homely scenes of everyday life. One of the greatest artists of all time was Rembrandt. He was a Dutchman. He loved to paint stories from the Bible. He had a great skill in painting people's emotions.

Today many artists are more interested in colours and patterns than in making 'photographic' paintings.

PANDA Deep in the bamboo forests of China lives the most famous of all animals. The giant panda is a wonderful black and white furry creature that looks rather like a bear. It lives only on the young shoots of the bamboo.

The giant panda is extremely rare now. Most of the forests where it lived have been cut down and it has been hunted for its lovely fur. Nobody knows how few pandas are left in the wild. A few live in zoos but captured pandas are not easy to breed. It may be too late to undo all the damage that has been done. Soon there may be no giant pandas left.

Giant panda

PAPER About two thousand years ago a Chinese man called Tsai Lun discovered how to make 'paper' by pressing plant fibres. The Ancient Egyptians, too, had a way of making papyrus from reeds. The word paper comes from the word papyrus.

Until recently paper was still made from grass plants and rags. Then it was discovered how to make it from wood-pulp. Wood-pulp comes from softwood trees, such as fir, pine and spruce. The trees are felled and the logs are taken to a pulp mill. They are put into a drum where the bark is rubbed off. Then they are made into pulp by grinding or by boiling with special chemicals. The pulp is then taken to the paper-mill and put into a big tub called a hydropulper. When the pulp is very 'sloppy', it is spread over a wire mesh belt. The water drains away through the mesh leaving a damp 'web' of paper. The web is pressed into a firm sheet by heavy rollers and dried as it passes through heated ones. At the end of the process the rough, dry web of paper goes through special heated rollers called *calendar presses*. These give it a nice, smooth surface.

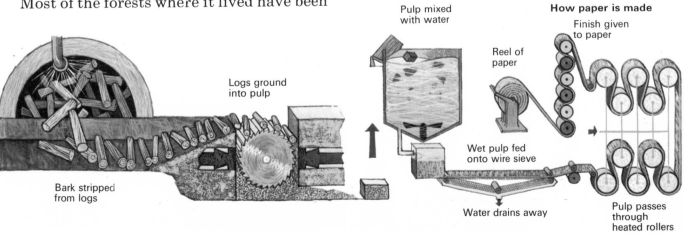

Pulp mixed with water

How paper is made

Finish given to paper

Reel of paper

Logs ground into pulp

Bark stripped from logs

Wet pulp fed onto wire sieve

Water drains away

Pulp passes through heated rollers

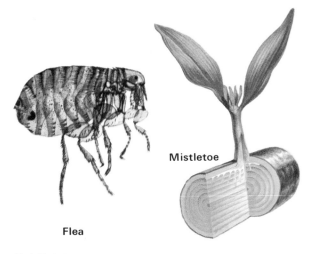

Mistletoe

Flea

PARASITES Mistletoe looks very pretty as a Christmas decoration but it is not a 'nice' plant. It 'steals' its food from the tree on which it grows. It is a parasite. It has no roots, so it takes water and salts from the tree to help make its food. The dodder is even worse. It has no roots or leaves. It twines round another plant, digs in its suckers and takes all its food from the plant. It usually kills the plant.

Some animals are also parasites. The plant or animal on which a parasite lives is called its host. Fleas and lice are parasites. They live on the skin or in the hair of their host and feed on its blood. Some parasites actually live inside their hosts. The tapeworm lives in the gut of its host and feeds on the digested food.

PARLIAMENT The name parliament comes from a French word meaning 'speaking'. In a Parliament members talk about or discuss and then pass new laws and taxes.

There are two Houses in the British Parliament. The Upper House or House of Lords is made up of Peers and Bishops. They are not elected. The House of Lords has few powers.

The members of the Lower House or House of Commons are elected or chosen by all citizens over the age of 18. They are elected every five years. There are three main parties in the House of Commons—Labour, Liberal, and Conservative. Each party has its own ideas on running the country. The party with the most members at an election forms the Government. The leader of the party becomes the Prime Minister. He chooses a team of ministers to govern with him—a minister of Education, a minister of Health, and so on. These ministers form the Cabinet. The Cabinet directs the Government.

PARROTS If you keep a parrot in a cage and look after it well, it may live for over 50 years. It may also learn to 'talk'. Parrots cannot really talk. They can only mimic the sounds people make. They cannot understand the words they say.

In the wild, parrots live in most of the warm parts of the world and especially in Australia. They usually live in flocks in forests, feeding on fruits, seeds and nuts. They perch in the tops of the trees and squawk all day with their loud, harsh voices.

Parrots are well known for the way they mimic the sounds people make

PEACOCK People are sometimes called 'as proud as peacocks'. Peacocks are very beautiful birds. The male peacock has a huge tail. The tail opens out like a fan. It is made of beautiful coloured feathers. When the peacock's tail is spread it walks very slowly. It does look very proud.

A peacock displaying its fan-shaped tail

PENGUINS In the southernmost part of the world is the huge continent of Antarctica. It is very cold and it is covered with ice and snow. This unfriendly country is the home of the penguin.

The penguin is a black and white bird. But it cannot fly. Instead it is a skilful

Peoples of the world differ greatly in their looks, their dress, and their way of life

swimmer and diver. Its short, powerful wings act as paddles in the water. Its feet are webbed. They help it to swim fast enough to catch fish.

On land penguins are clumsy. Their legs are very short and they waddle to and fro. Some penguins find it faster to slide down snowy slopes on their stomachs.

There are several different kinds of penguins. The largest are called the king penguin and the emperor penguins. These penguins do not make nests. They balance eggs on their feet to keep them from the snow. Their stomachs fold over the eggs to keep them warm. When the young penguins are very small they still spend a lot of their time on their parents' feet.

PEOPLES OF THE WORLD There are more than 3,500 million people in the world. They live in more than 130 countries, and speak almost 2,800 different languages. They vary a great deal in the colour of their eyes, their hair, and their skin. Their faces have many different shapes. But with all these variations, we can list them in three main groups. These groups consist of people with white skins, which scientists call *Caucasoid;* people with yellow skins, known as *Mongoloid;* and people with black skins, known as *Negroid.*

More than half the people of the world are Caucasoids. They include most of the people of Europe, India, North America, Australia, and New Zealand. About one third of the people are Mongoloids. They include the Chinese, Japanese, Red Indians, and Eskimos. The rest—about one person in every 10 of the world's people—are Negroids. They include the Negroes of Africa and some of the people who live on the small islands of the Pacific Ocean.

PERISCOPE A periscope is an instrument which is used for seeing around corners. It is a tube with a mirror at each end. The mirrors are at an angle to the tube, and exactly facing each other. When you look

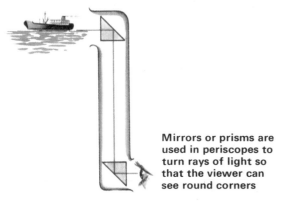

Mirrors or prisms are used in periscopes to turn rays of light so that the viewer can see round corners

at one mirror you see a reflection of the picture picked up by the other mirror. Periscopes are used in submarines under water to see what is happening above the surface. If you are in a crowd you can use a periscope to see over the heads of other people.

PETS Man's oldest companion and pet is the dog. This is because the dog is so useful —as a guard and a hunter. The dog is also very intelligent and a good companion. Cats, too, have been kept as pets for thousands of years. They were regarded as sacred in ancient Egypt. Cats and dogs are still the most popular pets.

Before deciding to keep a pet you must be prepared to look after it properly. Pets must be fed regularly. Some need constant exercise and frequent cleaning. You must also be willing to spare time to play with your pet each day. Neglect it, and it may become very lonely.

Caged birds such as canaries, parrots, and budgerigars need to have the right kind of food and temperature. It is wise to get a book on how to look after them.

Rabbits, mice, and guinea pigs make delightful pets. They all love company. So they should never be kept on their own.

Tortoises need very special care. When they go to sleep for the winter—*hibernate*— they must never be woken. They must also be kept in a warm place. In summer they enjoy foraging in the garden.

Some animals such as lambs, calves, and pigs, make amusing pets when they are young. Few are good pets when they grow up.

Whatever your pet, remember, it needs lots of care and lots of affection.

PIGS Someone once said that the only part of a pig that cannot be used is its grunt.

We eat its meat as bacon, pork, or sausages. Its fat is turned into lard. A pig's skin makes soft leather. Even its bristles are used to make brushes.

The male pig is called a boar. A female

A saddleback pig with her piglets

Scientists believe that the planets were formed from a cloud of gas and dust which whirled around the Sun

PLANETS In space there are nine large bodies that go round the Sun. They are called *planets*. The Earth is one of them. Like the Moon, the planets have no light of their own, but shine with light reflected from the Sun. The planet that is nearest to the Sun is called Mercury. The others, in order of distance, are Venus, Earth, Mars, Jupiter, Saturn, Uranus, Neptune, and Pluto. In 1972 astronomers (people who study the heavens) found what they thought was a tenth planet beyond Pluto. In addition to these major planets, there are about 2,000 tiny planets, called *asteroids*. They *orbit* (circle) the Sun midway between Mars and Jupiter.

The biggest planet is Jupiter, which is 11 times as big across as the Earth. Saturn is nearly as big as Jupiter. Mercury, less than half as big across as the Earth, is the smallest planet. As far as we can tell, none of the other planets has life on it like that on the Earth.

pig is called a sow. A sow usually gives birth to two litters of piglets a year. There may be from six to 12 piglets in each litter.

The Large White, the Berkshire, and the Danish Landrace are important breeds of modern pigs. Saddlebacks are so called because they have a belt of white hair.

The pig is descended from the wild boar. Wild boar are still found in parts of Europe. They are very strong and have sharp tusks.

Pigs cannot sweat. So, in hot weather, they wallow in mud to keep cool. Some people think pigs are dirty. In fact, they are very clean. They are also quite intelligent.

PIRATES For hundreds of years travel by sea was very dangerous. This was not just because of storms. There was also danger from pirates. Pirates were cruel sea robbers. They attacked ships and captured them. They stole their cargoes and robbed the travellers. Sometimes they captured important travellers and would not release them until large sums of money were paid.

The most famous pirates sailed in the Caribbean Sea. Ships with cargoes of gold sailed across the Caribbean Sea. They were taking the gold from South America to Spain. They were great prizes for pirates. Many pirates grew very rich.

Pirates flew a special flag which showed a skull above crossed bones. When sailors saw this flag they knew that the pirates were going to attack them.

Blackbeard was one of the most feared pirates. His real name was Edward Teach

PLASTICS Plastics are substances that can be easily shaped. We use many, many things made from plastics, such as toys, plates, pens, pipes, bottles, transparent bags, and even motor-car bodies. A plastic starts as a substance called a *resin*, which is made by chemists from coal, oil (petroleum), water, and other natural materials. The resin is in the form of powder or tiny pellets. In a plastics factory the resin is heated until it melts. Then it is poured or squeezed into moulds to make different shapes. Sheets and rods of plastics are made by squeezing them through a slit or hole—like you squeeze toothpaste out of the tube.

POETRY The very earliest poetry was recited. Sometimes it was sung. Like all poetry it had rhythm. The sounds made a pattern or design. Sometimes the pattern rhymed. The early poets usually composed poems about exciting battles or wars between gods. Some of their poems were so good that they were written down. The poetry of the Greek poet Homer was written down. He lived 3,000 years ago.

Later, poets wrote down the poems they composed. They wrote poems on all kinds of subjects. They wrote about love and nature and God. But not all poetry is solemn and serious. Some poets, like Chaucer and Swift, wrote amusing poems. They laughed at how silly people can be and how stupidly they sometimes behave.

Most people think that the greatest poet of all was William Shakespeare. He mainly wrote plays. But he wrote them as poetry— with rhythm. Some of his plays are sad and tragic. Hamlet and Macbeth are two very sad plays. Some of his plays are funny. Twelfth Night makes us laugh.

In some ways poets are like scientists. They experiment with words and the sounds they make. They try to find new ways of saying things with words. They also try to make words form exciting patterns. Like music and painting, poetry makes life more colourful and interesting.

POISON The stewed stems of rhubarb are very good to eat. But it is dangerous to eat rhubarb leaves. They contain poison.

Poisons are substances that make us ill. Some poisons can kill us. Many plants are

The berries of deadly nightshade are very poisonous

poisonous. So we should never eat any plant unless we are sure that it is not poisonous. Some animals have poisonous bites or stings. Snake bites can kill people. A wasp sting contains poison. It is painful to men. And it can kill some small creatures.

Poisons are not just found in plants and animals. Cleaning liquids like bleaches are poisonous. And many medicines are poisonous if you take too much. So never drink or eat anything unless you know it is quite safe.

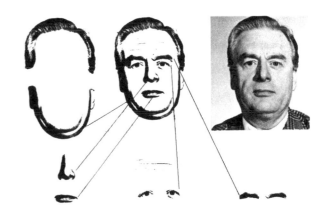

Policemen may make up a picture of the face of a suspect from descriptions by people who have seen him

POLICE Every country has laws to protect its people. And the men and women who make sure that these laws are kept are the police.

The main job of policemen is to prevent crimes. In towns and cities police patrol the streets on foot and in cars. They keep a sharp look out for anything unusual. And they are allowed to arrest people whom they think have broken the law.

When a crime takes place, specially trained policemen called detectives work to find out who did it. There are experts in the police force who can piece together what has happened with the help of complicated equipment.

The police help the people in many other ways. They direct the traffic. They help find things that people have lost. And if people are in trouble they can always ask a policeman what is the best thing to do.

PORTS AND HARBOURS When a ship reaches land it cannot just stop anywhere. It must find a place where it will be sheltered from storms and big waves. Places where ships can safely tie up, or berth, are called harbours.

The first harbours were well sheltered bays and inlets. Today most ships berth at specially built ports. They go to docks where their passengers and cargoes can easily be unloaded. Leading from the ports are good roads and railways which carry people and goods quickly inland. The ports have supplies of food and fuel and spare parts for the ships.

Some large ports have special docks where ships that have been damaged can be repaired. The ship goes through a narrow entrance which is shut behind it. Then the water in the dock is pumped out. Men can get to work on the damage.

At a busy port you can see ships unloading goods from many lands

POST OFFICE Men have always wanted to send messages. Once they had to be sent by runners, or horse messengers, or even by smoke signals. Now we can send letters and telegrams and make telephone calls to almost everywhere in the world. Each day millions of letters are posted. If they were all placed one on top of another the pile would be four times the height of Mount Everest. The Post Office has the job of delivering each of the letters and parcels to the correct address.

All the letters have to be collected, sorted and delivered. Once all the sorting was done by hand. Now there are big machines which sort them automatically. As soon as the letters are sorted, they are sent to all different parts of the country. Some go on

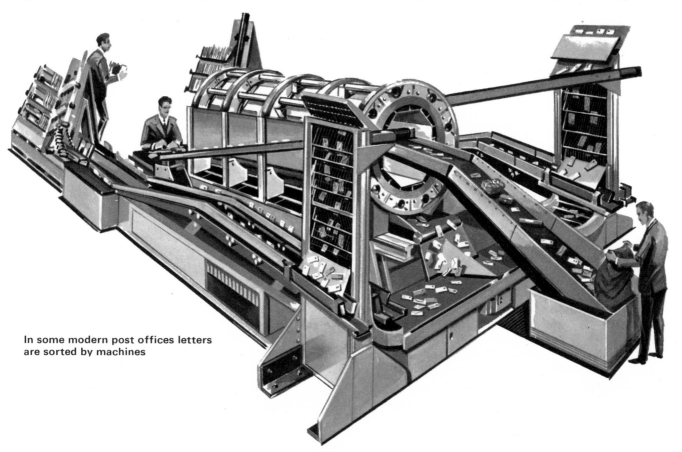

In some modern post offices letters are sorted by machines

Huge herds of buffalo once roamed the prairies of North America. Most of them were killed for food. The survivors were taken to a National Park for protection

You can make simple pots by coiling rolls of clay round and round, then smoothing them off

special mail trains which are like travelling post offices. The letters for each town are sorted as the train speeds on. Other letters and parcels have to be loaded on to ships and planes to go to other countries.

This all has to be done as fast as possible. No time is wasted, so that the postman can often deliver the letters the very next day.

POTTERY Thousands of years ago men discovered that they could make clay into all sorts of shapes. If they left it in the sun for a long time it would harden. Even if they put it in water it would not become soft again. They could make bowls and jugs for carrying water.

Sometimes they shaped the clay with their hands. Sometimes they coiled sausage-shaped pieces of clay round and round to make jars. Later they found that clay was

easiest to shape if they put in on a flat piece of wood which they spun round and round. They built ovens in which they baked their clay pots.

At first they decorated their pots by scratching them with sticks. Later they covered them with thin layers of coloured glazes. The glazes helped the pots to hold water. Many of the plates, mugs, and dishes we use today are made of pottery.

PRAIRIE In the centre of North America are vast grass-covered plains. They stretch for thousands of miles. When they were discovered by French explorers they were called prairies. This is the French word for grasslands.

The prairies are cold in winter. In summer it is hot and sometimes rainy. The grass grows quickly and in autumn it dries to hay. When settlers from Europe first went to the prairies wild buffaloes grazed there. The settlers reared huge herds of cattle. The herds were looked after by cowboys. Later they started huge wheat farms there.

PREHISTORIC ANIMALS History is the written story of what has happened in the world. Man has been able to write down the history of events for only about 5,000 years. We call the times before that *prehistoric*. Many strange animals lived in prehistoric times, a great many of them long before men existed. We know about these animals from *fossils*. Fossils are bones and shells that have been preserved in rocks, and have become like rocks themselves.

The earliest animals lived in the sea more than 600 million years ago. They were soft, jelly-like creatures. The first fishes came into existence about 500 million years ago. But about 100 million years passed before any animals started living on land. The first ones to do so were *amphibians*— creatures that live part of the time in water and the rest on land, as frogs do now.

The next creatures to evolve were *reptiles* —animals similar in type to our present-day snakes, lizards, and crocodiles. About 200 million years ago enormous reptiles which we call *dinosaurs* roamed the Earth. The biggest land animal that ever lived was a dinosaur we call *Brachiosaurus*. It stood

of the simplest ways of printing words is from little metal letters called type, which are arranged or "set" by machines like giant typewriters. The type is then made up into pages. A roller applies sticky ink to the type, and a piece of paper is pressed against the letters. The ink comes off on to the paper, leaving a perfect *impression* (copy) of the type. So that the impression is the right way round, the type has to be in reverse.

Printing pictures is rather different. One way is to photograph the picture through a screen so that it appears as a series of dots on a printing plate. Colour pictures, too, can be printed in this way, but the colours are first split into different shades of red, yellow, blue, and black. A separate printing plate is then made for each colour.

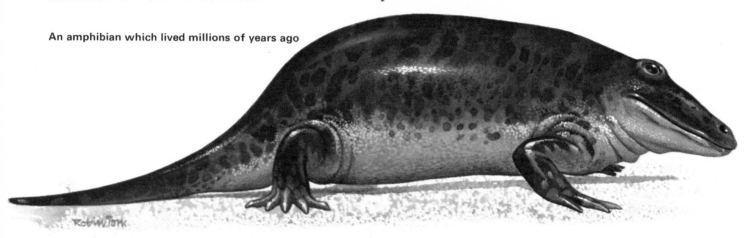

An amphibian which lived millions of years ago

higher than a two-storey house, and was about twice as long as a bus. The giant reptiles died out some time after the first mammals (warm-blooded animals) appeared. The first birds also appeared about the same time. The early mammals were tiny, mouselike creatures. But they gradually grew bigger. Finally, the first men appeared, about 500,000 years ago.

PRINTING Until just over 500 years ago people had to make copies of books and documents by writing them out by hand. But in the 1450s a German goldsmith, Johannes Gutenberg, invented printing—the art of making copies of books and other written matter by machinery. This invention made books cheap and available to all who wanted them. Before, they were rare and expensive.

There are different ways of printing. One

PRISM A piece of glass shaped like the roof of a house, with two triangular ends and three rectangular surfaces, is called a *prism*. A prism bends light that passes through it. For this reason, prisms can be used to take light round corners inside microscopes and binoculars—in much the same way as you can use a mirror to see round a corner. A prism can also be used to separate ordinary white light into a band of colours, called a *spectrum*.

Prism

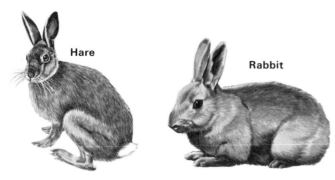

Hare

Rabbit

RABBITS AND HARES Although rabbits make wonderful pets and are valued for their fur and meat, in the wild they are pests. They live wild in most parts of the world, grazing on the grass with their long, front teeth. They also eat other green plants and do a lot of damage to farm crops.

Once there were no rabbits in Australia and New Zealand but a few were taken there. Soon there were millions of them and they ate nearly all the grass, leaving very little for the animals that lived there before.

Hares are near relatives of the rabbits. They are bigger and stronger and live in hollows in the ground instead of in burrows like the rabbits.

RADAR Ships and aeroplanes use radar to 'see' land and other objects through fog or darkness. Radar works by 'bouncing' radio waves off the object to be detected, just like an echo comes back to you, or a ball bounces back off a wall. By noting the time taken for the waves to come back, a radar operator can calculate how far away the object is. The radio 'echo' is shown on a screen like a miniature television screen.

The Italian inventor Marconi sent the first radio message across the Atlantic seventy years ago

RADIO Radio carries sound from one place to another by turning it into electrical waves that can travel long distances through space. The radio receiver you have in your home picks up these electrical waves and turns them back into sound waves again by means of a loudspeaker. Radio waves travel only in straight lines. To get them to go round the curve of the Earth, they have to be 'bounced' off a satellite, or off part of the Earth's atmosphere called the *ionosphere*, which acts as a mirror for some kinds of radio waves. It is possible to send radio signals to the Moon and other objects in space. Scientists are now studying mysterious radio signals that appear to be coming to us from far distant stars.

RAILWAYS For hundreds of years people relied on horses and stage coaches when they went on journeys. They had to put up with bad roads and fear of highwaymen. Then the steam engine was invented but it could not be used on the rough roads. A man called Richard Trevithick first realised that the rails which were used to carry horse-drawn carts in coal mines could be used to carry locomotives.

The first railway line was built in 1825 to carry coal between Stockton and Darlington. George Stephenson built the line and its first engine, *Locomotion*. He also built the first line on which people travelled. It ran between Liverpool and Manchester and the carriages were pulled by the *Rocket*.

A diesel locomotive

Steel rails are clipped to plates which rest on wooden or concrete sleepers

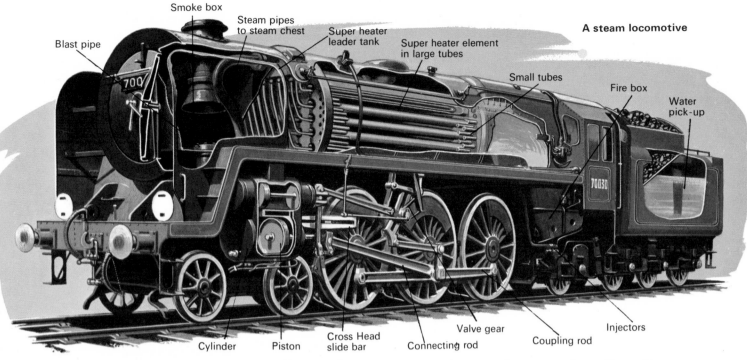

Blast pipe · Smoke box · Steam pipes to steam chest · Super heater leader tank · Super heater element in large tubes · Small tubes · Fire box · Water pick-up

Cylinder · Piston · Cross Head slide bar · Connecting rod · Valve gear · Coupling rod · Injectors

Soon railways were spreading all over the world. In England an engineer called Brunel designed marvellous bridges and tunnels to carry the lines. In America work was started on a great railway that would run right across the country. Work was started from the Atlantic and Pacific coasts and in 1869 the two tracks met.

Although the first railways were built for steam trains, today nearly all railway engines are electric or diesel locomotives. They are faster and cheaper than steam.

In some countries railways are built that run on a single track called a monorail. The train hangs from a line which may run right over the roads. On Japan's New Tokkaido line the train travels like a bullet over a normal track. It runs at over 100 m.p.h.

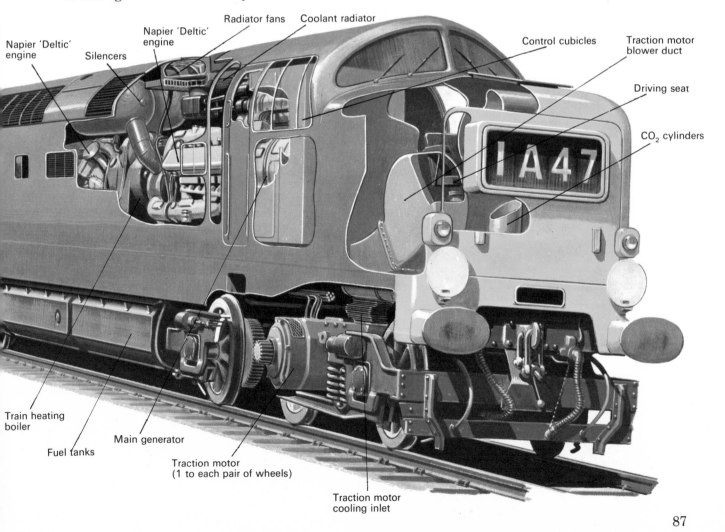

Napier 'Deltic' engine · Silencers · Napier 'Deltic' engine · Radiator fans · Coolant radiator · Control cubicles · Traction motor blower duct · Driving seat · CO$_2$ cylinders

Train heating boiler · Fuel tanks · Main generator · Traction motor (1 to each pair of wheels) · Traction motor cooling inlet

RAIN Rain is little drops of water that fall from clouds in the sky. It soaks into the ground, providing water for trees and other plants to drink. Some of it flows out of the ground again and down hillsides to form rivers. The rivers flow into lakes or into the sea. From lakes and rivers we get the water we drink. When the Sun shines on lakes and the sea it heats up some of the water and turns it into water vapour, which is rather like steam. This vapour rises into the sky and forms into clouds again.

RAINBOW Although sunlight looks white, it is really made up of 'all the colours of the rainbow'. There are in fact seven colours— red, orange, yellow, green, blue, indigo, and violet. A rainbow is made when sunlight shines through millions of raindrops. As sunlight enters each raindrop the light is bent and reflected. In doing this, the raindrop breaks the sunlight up into the colours of which it is formed. Each of the seven colours comes out at a different angle.

RATS AND MICE The rat and the mouse are rodents. Most of them are pests which have followed man to almost every corner of the world. The house-mouse sleeps in quiet places during the day and raids kitchens and larders for food at night.

Rats are much bigger than mice and they do more damage. They damage food stores and buildings and spread diseases. The black rat is over a foot long and its tail is half its length. It often lives in ships' holds where the cargo is stored.

Rats and mice breed very quickly. For years people used cats and traps to catch them but now poison is used. Not all rats and mice are pests. The harvest mouse is a gentle little animal that lives in corn fields. Special white mice are bred as pets and white rats are bred for use in medical research.

Harvest mouse

House mouse

RECORDING One hundred years ago no-one had heard the sound of his own voice as others hear it. Then the great American inventor Thomas Alva Edison built a machine that recorded sound. He called it a 'phonograph', which means 'sound writer'. And that is what it was. A needle, vibrated by the voice, cut a wavy groove in a piece of

When air rises and cools, some of the invisible water vapour it contains turns back to little drops of water. These float in the air as clouds. If a lot of vapour turns back to water the drops grow too big to float in the air. They fall to the ground as rain

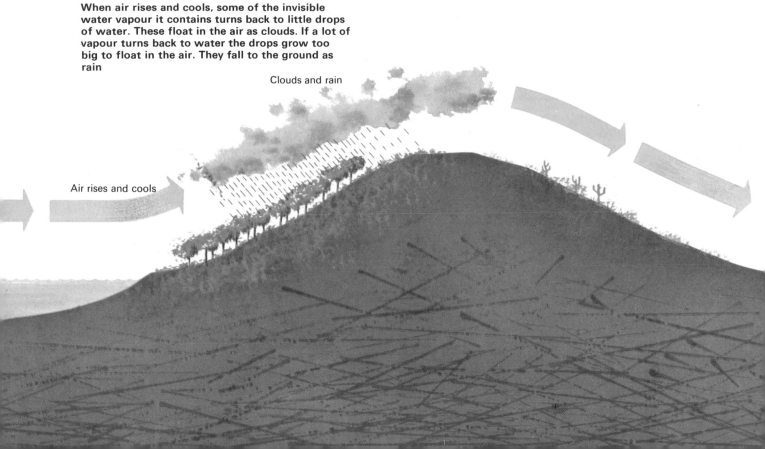

Clouds and rain

Air rises and cools

tin foil or in wax on a revolving cylinder. Putting the needle back in the groove on the cylinder reproduced the sound of the voice.

Our modern record player developed from the phonograph. Now, of course, recording and playing back are done electrically. And the recording is made on a disc, not a cylinder. But it still uses the idea of a wavy groove and a vibrating needle.

We now have other ways of recording sound, such as the tape recorder in which sounds are recorded on magnetic tape. The sound for films is recorded as a pattern of light on the same strip of film as the pictures.

RED CROSS Just over one hundred years ago the armies of France and Austria fought a terrible battle in northern Italy. When it was over a young Swiss banker named Henri Dunant visited the battlefield. He saw thousands of wounded soldiers with no one to care for them.

When Henri Dunant returned to Switzerland he begged the nations of the world to agree to help the victims of war. A few years later the Red Cross was set up. This organization is recognised by the nations of the world. Its aim is to help the victims of war or disasters. The sign of the organization is the reverse of the Swiss flag—a red cross on a white background.

REFRIGERATOR We can keep food fresh for a time by cooling it in a refrigerator. Cooling slows down the processes which make food go bad.

When a liquid turns to a gas it takes in, or absorbs, heat. A refrigerator works by sending a special liquid through pipes in the food compartment and making it turn to a gas. As the liquid turns to gas it absorbs heat from the food. In this way the food is cooled. The gas is turned back to a liquid in another part of the refrigerator.

REINDEER Most deer are wild animals which shy away from people. But one sort of deer has been herded by men for hundreds of years. This is the reindeer. It lives in the cold northern parts of Europe. It has a woolly coat and both the male reindeer and the female reindeer have wide, branching antlers.

The reindeer are kept in herds like cows.

Reindeer

They are herded by people called Lapps. The reindeer provide them with milk and meat. Their skins are used for clothing. And reindeer can be trained to pull sledges quickly across the snow.

Reindeer also live in North America. There they are called caribou.

RELIGION Since the earliest times people have believed in one god or in more than one god. They have worked out ways of worshipping their god or gods. They have worked out a way of life—what is right and what is wrong. And they have worked out what happens after death. Their beliefs and their ways of worshipping make up their religion.

There have been many religions in the history of the world. And there are many religions in the world today. Some religions have only a few followers. Other religions have millions of followers. Buddhism, Christianity, Hinduism, Islam and Judaism are some of the greatest religions. Together they include over half the people in the world.

In the past wars have been fought to make people worship in a certain way. And people have suffered because of their beliefs. Now people are learning to respect each other's ideas and beliefs.

REPTILES Lizards, snakes, crocodiles and turtles are all reptiles. They are cold-blooded animals with scaly skins and they hatch from eggs like birds.

There was a time when reptiles ruled the Earth. The great dinosaurs were reptiles and so were the pterosaurs that flew in the air. But these creatures died out suddenly. Today, reptiles are smaller, although the anaconda snake and some of the giant crocodiles grow to a length of 30 feet. Because they are cold-blooded, reptiles do not live in really cold places. In places where the winters are cold, they hibernate.

Turtles, tortoises and terrapins have strong shells to protect them. When in danger, the tortoise can quickly pull its legs and head into the safety of its shell.

Snakes have no arms or legs but they can move very easily by pressing their scales against the ground. They are also quick to catch their prey. Some crush their victims by coiling themselves round animals until they die. Others inject their victims with poison from their fangs. But most snakes are quite harmless.

Lizards have many different ways of catching their prey and of escaping from their enemies. The chameleon has a long, sticky tongue which it shoots out to catch insects, and, like many other lizards, it is safe from its enemies because the colour of its skin changes to match its background.

Crocodiles and alligators live by the banks of tropical rivers. They float in the water with their nostrils just above the surface, waiting for their prey. On land they are just as lazy, lying with their mouths open in the hot sun.

RHINOCEROS The rhinoceros is built like a great armoured tank. It has one or two horns on its nose and its thick hide hangs in folds from its body. It lives on grasslands in Africa and Asia and feeds only on plants.

The rhinoceros's only real enemy is man. It is too well-armoured and fierce for other animals to attack. But for years people have hunted the rhinoceros. They believed that its horn had the power to stop them growing old. Now several kinds of rhinoceros are very rare indeed.

Tortoise

Thorny Devil

Anaconda

Diamond-Back Rattlesnake

Python

Cobra

Leaf-nosed snake

RIVERS When rain falls on the land it seeps down through the ground. The water collects together when it reaches a layer of hard rock. It comes back to the surface as a spring. Many little springs join together to form a river.

Many rivers start in hills or mountains. They flow quickly downhill. Later they reach flatter country. There they join up with other rivers. They flow more slowly and many are very wide. In the end they flow into a lake or into the sea.

The earliest men settled beside rivers. The rivers gave them water for themselves and for their crops and animals. The men could eat the fish that swam in the rivers. And often, when the country was difficult to travel across, they rowed or sailed from one riverside village to another.

Today rivers are still very useful to men. They provide water for us to drink and for our farms. Some rivers are so large that huge ships can travel up and down them.

Many rivers start in mountains. They flow through steep valleys and over waterfalls. When they reach flatter country, rivers flow in great loops over the land. Some rivers enter the sea through a delta made of soil washed from the land

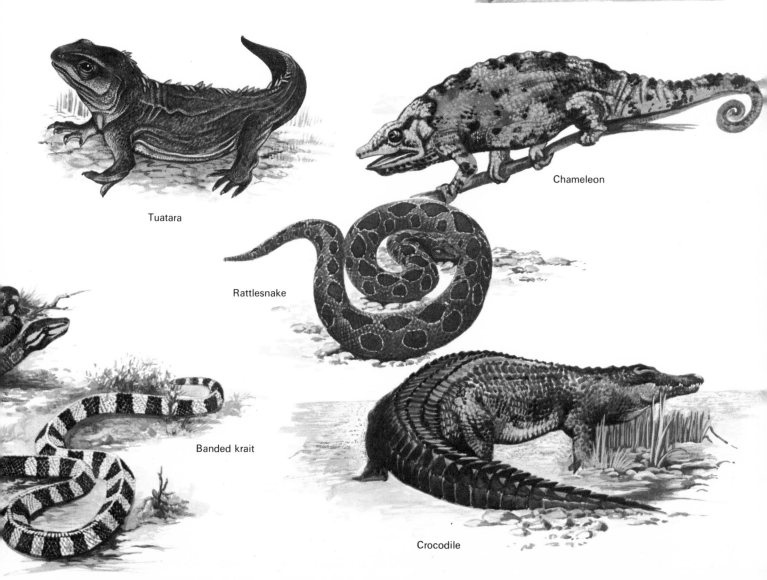

Tuatara

Chameleon

Rattlesnake

Banded krait

Crocodile

ROADS Today the countryside is criss-crossed by roads. They make it easy for us to visit places many miles away by car or by bus. Large cities are linked by specially wide roads. These roads are designed so that people can travel very fast on them. They are called motorways.

The first great road builders were the Romans. Hundreds of years ago they built long, straight roads between the cities of their huge empire. They built their roads very well. First they had a layer of large stones. They covered the large stones with small stones. The top layer was of large paving stones. Along these roads their armies could march easily. Their fast chariots rolled swiftly over the smooth surface.

When the Roman empire collapsed no one bothered to look after the roads. So for hundreds of years roads were tracks of bare earth. The wheels of carts and carriages made deep ruts in them. In dry weather travellers were surrounded by clouds of choking dust. In wet weather they sometimes had to get out and help push the carriages through the thick mud.

About two hundred years ago people started once again to make roads of stone.

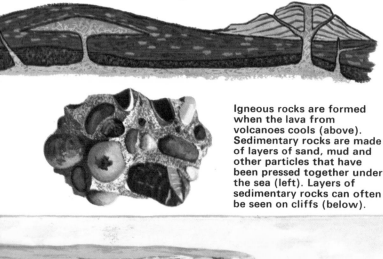

Igneous rocks are formed when the lava from volcanoes cools (above). Sedimentary rocks are made of layers of sand, mud and other particles that have been pressed together under the sea (left). Layers of sedimentary rocks can often be seen on cliffs (below).

Today the first stage of road building is to make the ground firm and flat. Then several layers of crushed stone are laid down. Last comes a top layer. Sometimes it is made of concrete. Sometimes it is made of little stones held together by tar.

Beaver   Squirrel

Rodents have a pair of strong front teeth for gnawing. These teeth grow as fast as they are worn away

ROCK The Earth's *crust*—that is, the outer layer we live on and sink mines into —is made up of rock or stone. A great deal of this rock is covered with a thin layer of soil, in which plants grow. But you can often see rocks exposed on seaside cliffs and mountain sides.

There are three main types of rocks. The first, which we call *igneous*, is made of molten material from deep in the Earth which has come to the surface and hardened, like toffee. A good example of igneous rock is granite, a very hard stone. The second type of rock we call *sedimentary*. It is formed by layers of little particles of rock and other materials. These particles settled on the ocean floor, just as the particles in a jar of muddy water will settle if you leave them. In time, these particles became hard rock. Sandstone and chalk are examples. The third kind of rock is called *metamorphic*. It consists of rock of the other two kinds that has been changed by heat or pressure. Slate is an example.

ROCKETS The rockets we light as fireworks and the rockets that carry astronauts to the Moon work in the same way. Fuel burns inside the rocket's tail to produce a hot gas. This gas expands. As it does so, it pushes on the body of the rocket and drives it forward, and a jet of hot gas escapes at the back. Space rockets use a great deal of fuel, which is heavy and bulky to carry. For this reason, they are made in sections, known as stages. The first stage blasts the rocket off the ground. When its fuel is used it is discarded, and the second stage carries the rocket still higher. Finally, the third stage takes the rocket into space on its way to the Moon or one of the planets.

RODENTS More than half the mammals in the world are rodents. These are small animals with large chisel-shaped front teeth which grow as fast as they are worn away. Beavers, squirrels, chipmunks, porcupines and rats and mice are just a few of the rodents. They are mostly only small animals but they have survived because they breed so fast. Despite man's efforts to kill off the rat, there are still more rats in the world than people.

The first 'space' rockets were weapons of war. They carried bombs high above the ground and landed hundreds of miles away. Some rockets are still made to carry bombs to distant countries. But the largest rockets are made for space exploration. The Saturn moon rocket is as tall as a skyscraper

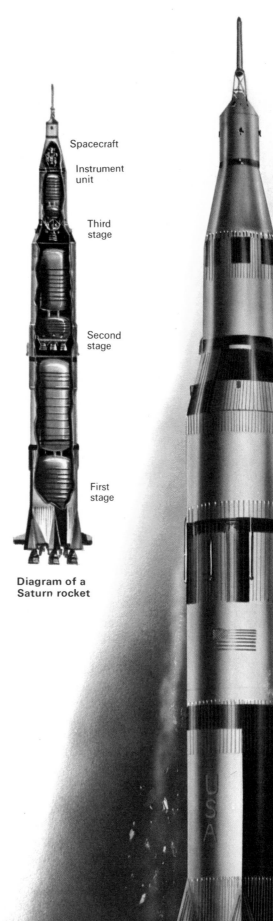

Diagram of a Saturn rocket

Spacecraft

Instrument unit

Third stage

Second stage

First stage

V-2   Mercury-   Saturn 1   Vostok   Saturn 5
       Atlas

A Saturn rocket blasting-off

ROME, ANCIENT In Britain and all over Europe you can still travel on roads that were first built by the Romans. The Romans built these roads so that they could quickly reach any part of their huge empire. This empire stretched from the borders of Scotland in the north to the deserts of Saudi Arabia. This empire was kept in order and ruled by the army and by a wise system of government.

The army was divided into units. A hundred men made up a century, six centuries a cohort, and ten cohorts a legion. The soldiers were very well trained. The huge Roman empire was divided into provinces. Each province was ruled by a governor. The capital of the empire was the magnificent city of Rome. Here can be seen the remains of many splendid buildings put up by skilled builders and engineers. In the Forum, or market place, you can still see the ruins of the Senate (the Roman parliament) as well as those of temples and triumphal arches. Fine Roman buildings such as aqueducts and villas (houses) and baths are still standing in all parts of Europe and the Middle East.

Latin, the language of ancient Rome, was spoken all over the empire. Many modern languages are descended from it—Italian, Spanish, and French, for example. And for centuries—almost to the present day—Latin was the 'language of learning'.

The Romans copied much of their art and literature and religion from Greece. They are mostly remembered for being great builders and engineers, fine soldiers, and good rulers.

The Roman army was very well trained. It was better than any other army at that time. Roman foot soldiers fought mainly with short, flat swords. The Roman soldiers were helped by auxiliaries. Auxiliaries were troops from conquered lands

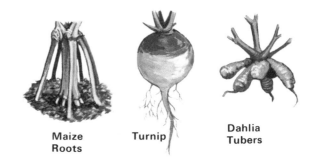

Maize Roots | Turnip | Dahlia Tubers

ROOT CROPS Some plants store food in underground stems called tubers or in their roots. These plants are grown specially for food. Many vegetables are root crops. They are good to eat because they contain starch which gives us energy.

The best-known root vegetable is the potato. Once it grew only in South America. Now it is grown all over the world. We also eat swedes, turnips, mangels, carrots, parsnips, radishes and beetroots. In hotter countries the yam, the cassava and the sweet potato are important root crops.

The most important sweet root crop is the sugar beet. It is grown in many of the cooler parts of the world. Arrowroot and liquorice are also root crops.

ROOTS A plant's roots are very important. They hold the plant firmly in the ground and

Legionary | Centurion | Standard bearer | Auxiliary

they take in water and minerals from the soil. The plant needs these to make its food in its leaves.

There are two kinds of roots. The tap root is a big main root from which a few small branches grow. A carrot is a tap root. Fibrous roots are a mass of fine roots which grow from the bottom of the plant stem. Grass has fibrous roots.

Roots grow at the tip. Behind the tip there are tiny hairs which absorb the water and salts from the soil.

Many plants use their roots to store food for use when they cannot make enough in their leaves. We often eat these roots as they contain good food.

Rose

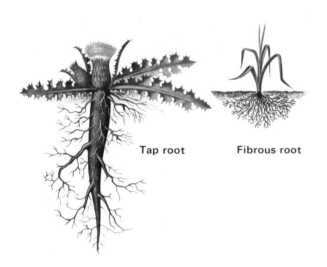

Tap root   Fibrous root

ROSE The national flower of England is the rose. Many roses grow wild in the hedges. They have five pale pink petals. Roses grown in gardens are much larger. They have many petals and may be many different colours. Most roses smell very sweet.

Hundreds of years ago two powerful groups of English noblemen quarrelled. One group, the Yorkists, chose a white rose as its emblem. The other group, the Lancastrians, chose a red rose. Their struggles are known as the Wars of the Roses. These wars ended when a new king, Henry Tudor, came to the throne. The Tudors chose a red and white rose as their emblem.

RUBBER The tyres of a car must be very strong. They must be airtight so that they can be blown up. They must be waterproof so that the car can safely drive through

puddles. They must be flexible so that they give a little when they go over rough stones. And they must be able to last a long time. There is only one material that is good enough to make tyres. It is called rubber.

Rubber comes from trees. These rubber trees grow in hot damp countries like those of South America and South-East Asia. If you cut the bark of a rubber tree a milky fluid called latex flows out. The latex is collected and acid is added to it. This turns it solid. Now men have learnt to make artificial rubber too.

Rubber is used for many things besides tyres. Balls are made of rubber because it bounces. Because rubber stretches easily it is made into elastic. Cloth coated with rubber is waterproof. And we use little pieces of rubber to 'rub out' pencil marks.

Tapping a rubber tree

Iron rusts when it is left out in the rain

SALT The table salt we use to season our food is one of a very large group of chemicals called salts. The scientific name of table salt is sodium chloride. Sodium chloride is found in the sea together with many other salts. It is also found in some rocks. To remain healthy all animals must eat a certain amount of salt.

RUST When iron is left out in the rain it soon becomes covered with a layer of reddish-brown rust. This flakes off and more rust forms. Slowly the metal is eaten away.

Rusting is caused by the oxygen in the air and by moisture. Together they attack the metal. Neither causes rusting on its own.

The layer of 'rust' which forms on aluminium and chromium does not flake off, so the metal under the surface is not eaten away. These metals are often used to cover other metals and protect them from rusting.

SALMON The salmon is an important food fish which leads a very unusual life. It starts its life in a quiet stream at the head of the river. After about a year it swims down river to the sea where it spends several years. Then one day the salmon starts a hard and wonderful journey back to the place where it was born. Often the journey is thousands of miles long. The salmon travels against the flow of the river, jumping rapids and waterfalls and being dashed against the rocks. At the end of the journey it is worn out and has lost its colour. It lays its eggs on the stream bed and then drifts away from the nest. Usually it is so tired that it dies.

Communications satellite

SATELLITES Satellites are objects in space that travel round and round a planet. The Moon is a satellite, because it travels round the Earth. Five other planets also have satellites. They are Jupiter, which has 12, Saturn, which has 10, Uranus, which has 5, and Mars and Neptune, which have 2 each. These satellites are sometimes called *moons,* after our Moon.

Artificial satellites are man-made objects that go round the Earth. There are several hundreds of them, and each of them has a special job to do. Some of them help to transmit (send) radio and television signals from one side of the Earth to the other. They are called *communications satellites.* Others include *weather satellites,* which take TV pictures of clouds and storms; *military satellites,* which take TV pictures of other countries' armies and weapons; and *scientific satellites,* which carry instruments to measure and record information that is of use to scientists.

SCAVENGERS These creatures are nature's dustmen. They feed on dead animals or on animal waste such as dung. Without them the world would be one big rubbish dump.

Salmon

Vultures

Many insects are scavengers, especially beetles and flies. They often lay their eggs on the dead bodies of animals and the larvae eat the flesh when they hatch.

The biggest scavengers are the jackals and hyenas and the great flesh-eating birds, the vultures, which quickly pick all the flesh from the bones of dead animals.

Most important of all scavengers are the ones we cannot see—the bacteria and other microscopic scavengers which break down all living things when they die.

Scorpion

SCORPION In hot countries people shake out their shoes and clothes before they put them on in case there is a scorpion hiding in them. The scorpion is an eight-legged creature related to the spiders. It eats insects, spiders and other small animals. It catches them with its great pincers. When it is attacked the scorpion has another weapon. It has a powerful sting in the end of the long tail which arches over its back. A scorpion sting is very painful but it is not usually strong enough to kill a man.

SCULPTURE Most of the very earliest sculpture was made for use in religious ceremonies. People made idols to please their gods or to drive away evil spirits. The Egyptians and, above all, the Greeks were the greatest sculptors of the ancient world. The Greeks greatly admired the beauty of the human body. Many of their statues show athletes in action. The Greeks also made statues of their gods and heroes. And they used sculpture to decorate buildings.

In Christian times sculpture was used to adorn churches and cathedrals and to honour the famous.

Modern sculptors—like Henry Moore, for example—are less interested in copying nature. They try more to make their sculpture form beautiful patterns or express ideas.

There are two main kinds of sculpture: *carving* and *moulding*. In carving the sculptor cuts into the wood, stone, ivory, or whatever material he is using. In moulding the sculptor makes his model with soft clay. He then bakes the clay to harden it. From the model he may then make a mould. Into the mould he then pours concrete or hot metal (bronze or silver, for example). Today sculptors sometimes weld pieces of metal into beautiful shapes.

Tools for carving

The shore-crab has powerful claws. It waves its claws around when it is angry

SEALS Have you seen a sea lion in a circus or a zoo? These clever water animals can learn all sorts of tricks. They are members of the seal family.

Seals spend most of their time in the sea. Their smoothly shaped bodies allow them to swim swiftly. Their legs have changed to flippers which help them to move through the water. Under their skins they have a thick layer of fat called blubber. This keeps them warm when they are swimming in cold water.

Each year seals come ashore to raise their young. On land they are clumsy. Some of them waddle about on their flippers. But others can only slither around on their stomachs.

Baby seal

SEASHORE The seashore is the place where the land meets the sea. The shore plants and animals lead unusual lives. Sometimes, when the tide is in, they are covered by the sea and sometimes they are left uncovered. There are also many different kinds of beaches. Some are sandy, some are muddy and some are rocky.

A sandy beach looks empty when the tide is out. This is because most of the animals have buried themselves in the sand to get away from the hot sun. Worms and the tiny shelled animals have to keep their bodies moist.

The water does not sink so quickly on muddy beaches when the tide goes out. Shrimps and small crabs are often left in the muddy water.

But the best beaches to explore for animals are the rocky shores. Many sea creatures are left in rock pools when the tide goes out. There are barnacles, sea-anemones, winkles, limpets, shrimps and fishes. The anemones and barnacles are closed when the tide is out but when it comes in they open up and put out their 'arms' to catch food.

Many animals hide under the seaweed to escape the sun and their enemies. Sometimes there is so much seaweed that you can hardly see the rocks, but when you move the seaweed all sorts of fishes and small creatures dart out.

Around the beach and on the cliffs there are the homes of many sea birds. There are gulls, gannets and cormorants. The puffins dig burrows in the cliffs with their feet.

Some beaches are made completely of shells. There are many different kinds and each one has a different shape. They are well worth collecting.

As the Earth travels around the Sun first one pole and then the other leans towards the Sun. This is why there are different seasons

SEASONS The seasons are the different times of the year that we call spring, summer, autumn, and winter. Spring is the time when trees sprout new leaves, and plants begin to grow. Summer is the hottest time of the year, when all the flowers are out. In autumn we harvest the crops, and the leaves fall off the trees—which is why some people call autumn *fall*. Winter is the coldest time of the year. In the northern part of the world, spring is in March, April and May, but in the southern part autumn begins then, and spring starts in September. Near the Equator, the imaginary line round the middle of the Earth, there are generally only two seasons. One is dry, with little or no rain. The other is wet, with a great deal of rain.

Seasons are caused by the way that the Earth travels round, or orbits, the Sun. The Earth is like a tilted top spinning through space. At one point in the orbit the North Pole leans towards the Sun and northern

lands have their summer while southern lands have their winter. At the opposite point in the orbit the South Pole leans towards the Sun and southern lands have their summer while northern lands have their winter. Spring and autumn are the points in the orbit when the tilt of the Earth is sideways on to the Sun. Northern and southern lands have similar amounts of warmth from the Sun.

SEAWEEDS Seaweeds belong to the simplest group of plants—the algae. They have no flowers.

There are three types of seaweed: red, green and brown. Green seaweeds grow high up the beach. Brown seaweeds grow further down. One famous brown seaweed is the bladderwrack or 'popweed'. It has little bulbs on its fronds which 'pop' when you squeeze them. Further down the shore is the red seaweed which can live even in deep water.

The biggest seaweeds, the kelps and oarweeds, are sometimes over 50 feet long.

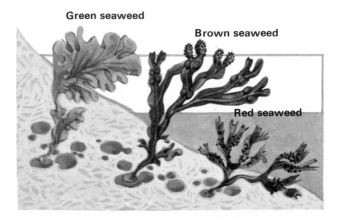

SEEDS If all seeds fell directly below the parent plant, there would not be room for them to grow. But plants have developed all sorts of different ways of spreading their seeds far around them.

Many seeds are scattered by the wind. Some, like dandelion seeds, float through the air on feathery down. Trees like the sycamore have seeds with a kind of wing attached, so that they glide along. The seed head of a poppy looks rather like a pepper pot. There are little holes running round just below the top edge. When the poppy head is swayed by the wind the seeds are shaken out.

Some seeds, like those of the pea and bean family, grow in pods. When the pods get really dry, they suddenly split open and the seeds are shot out. On a hot day you can sometimes hear the noise of these exploding seed pods.

Many seeds are carried away by animals. Some have little hooks which catch onto the coats of passing animals or people. Fruits and berries are eaten by birds who scatter the seeds miles away.

SENSES How do we know what is happening all round us? We are told by our senses. We have five senses. We *see* with our eyes. We *hear* with our ears. We *smell* with our noses. We *taste* with our mouths. And our skin feels anything it *touches*. All these parts of our bodies send messages to our brain which tells us what is going on.

Our sense of touch is very special. We can feel whether something is rough or smooth. We can also feel whether it is hot

The seeds of many flowers are spread by animals. Birds eat berries, squirrels eat acorns and ants take home seeds to feed their young. Sometimes these animals drop seeds on the ground. Then new plants can grow. Prickly burrs that contain seeds stick to the fur of animals. The burrs may be carried a long way before they drop to the ground

Pyramids

Hanging Gardens of Babylon

Temple of Artemis (Diane)

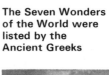
The Seven Wonders
of the World were
listed by the
Ancient Greeks

Statue of Zeus

Colossus of Rhodes

Mausoleum at Halicarnassus

Pharos of Alexandria

or cold. And if we cut ourselves we feel pain. The tiny nerve endings in our skin can tell the difference, and they send different messages back to our brain.

Most animals have these five senses. Many of them are much better than ours. Bats have specially good hearing. Dogs can smell many things that we cannot.

SEVEN WONDERS OF THE WORLD You could probably make a long list of the world's great 'tourist attractions'. It might include the Tower of London, the Eiffel Tower, the Taj Mahal, and so on. Like people today, the ancient Greeks were great travellers. They made a list of the greatest sights or 'tourist attractions' of the ancient world. These sights have become known as the Seven Wonders of the World. They are: 1. The pyramids or tombs of the pharaohs. 2. The Hanging Gardens of Babylon. These were probably gardens built on terraces of a tall tower. 3. The Colossus of Rhodes. This was an enormous statue of the sun-god Helios. It stood at the entrance of the harbour to the island of Rhodes. 4. The Pharos of Alexandria. This was a lighthouse which towered to a height of 400 feet. It stood at the entrance of Alexandria harbour. 5. The magnificent Temple of Artemis near the city of Ephesus. 6. The Statue of the God Zeus by the Greek sculptor Phidias. 7. The Mausoleum at Halicarnassus. This was the tomb of a ruler called Mausolus.

SHARKS The most feared of all fishes are the sharks, even though most of them are harmless to man. Sharks look very fierce. They have large, blunt heads with rows of sharp teeth and a large fin sticking up from their backs. It is often the sight of this fin cutting through the water that warns people that they could be in danger.

Some sharks are only the size of herrings but some kinds grow to a length of 45 feet. The largest shark is the whale shark. It is the largest of all fishes.

There are only a few man-eating sharks. The white shark, the blue shark, the tiger shark and the leopard shark are all very dangerous.

Sharks differ from other fishes because they do not have hard bones. Like the skates and rays their bones are 'soft'. They are made of cartilage like peoples' ears.

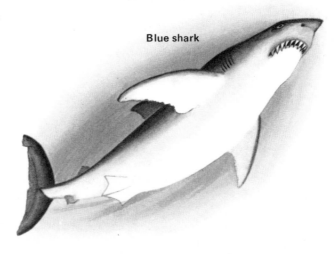
Blue shark

Scottish Blackface   Merino

Wensleydale   Suffolk

SHEEP Men have kept flocks of sheep for thousands of years. They have spun their wool for clothing, eaten their meat (lamb and mutton), and made their milk into cheese.

The male sheep is called a *ram*. The female sheep is called a *ewe*. Sheep are easy animals to keep. They can be simply left to graze on large areas of grassland. On the sheep stations of Australia and New Zealand the flocks often number thousands of sheep.

Today, sheep are usually bred either for their meat or for their wool. Merino sheep, for example, are reared for their fine wool. Many famous breeds of sheep are named after parts of Britain—Cheviot, Dorset Horn, and Suffolk sheep, for example.

Some of the many different kinds of shell.

SHELLS Have you ever collected shells by the seashore? They come in all sorts of shapes and sizes. There are the cone-shaped shells of limpets that cling to the rocks. There are shells that coil round in a spiral, like the shells of garden snails. There are saucer-shaped shells. All these shells belong to soft-bodied creatures. They protect them from harm. Some creatures, like crabs and lobsters, even have legs covered with jointed shells.

The animals that live inside these shells do not have bones inside their bodies. The shells take the place of skeletons. But some animals have skeletons *and* shells. Tortoises and turtles are like this. Their shells are made of horny plates and, like other shells, they keep the soft-bodied animals inside them safe.

SHIPS Perhaps, long ago, a prehistoric man sat on a floating log and realised how to make a boat. Probably the first boats were simple tree trunks with a hollow made in them. The early Egyptians made raft-like boats from strong reeds lashed together. The early Britons made coracles of animal skins stretched across a wooden frame.

All the early boats were driven by paddles or oars. Then people realised that it was much easier to let the wind do the hard work. Boats with sails could be made bigger and heavier and could sail across the sea.

Boats with oars as well as sails were still used for speed and power. The Romans had warships called galleys. They sometimes had two or three banks of oars and had a deadly ram at the front. They carried many soldiers and slaves to row them. The Phoenicians and Ancient Greeks also had trading boats and warships with oars and sails. The Vikings were probably the last people to use warships like these. Their longships had high prows with fearsome dragon's heads carved on them. They must have been a terrifying sight to the peaceful nations they raided.

Later new sorts of sails were discovered which enabled ships to sail into the wind as well as with it. Soon ships had more and more masts and sails. Some of the great trading ships and warships built during the time of King Henry VIII had two or three masts and many different kinds of sails.

The great ships-of-the-line, like Nelson's ship, *Victory*, carried between 65 and 100 guns. They were strongly built but could not sail like the *'clippers'*. These ships raced home from the East with cargoes of tea and spices. They were much faster than the *frigates* and *East-Indiamen* which carried cargoes of food and arms.

The great sailing ships were soon replaced when steamships were invented. They were driven by paddle wheels at first and then by propellers like modern ships. They were also now being built of metal instead of wood. One of the most famous of the early steamships was Brunel's *Great Eastern*.

Today, ships are built of steel and are usually powered by oil or even nuclear power. Some of the biggest ships are tankers built to carry tons of oil round the world.

Ships now also have all sorts of instruments on them to help the crew. They have radio, radar, depth-sounders and even the steering can be done by an automatic pilot. The new passenger liners have special fins on the sides to stop the ship rolling in rough seas.

SILK In many parts of the world are special caterpillar farms. The caterpillars are called silkworms, because they produce the lovely fibres that are woven into silk.

The Egyptians made boats from bundles of reeds. Later they used wood to make their boats

Viking longships had a square sail which could be used when the wind was blowing in the right direction

A Medieval ship with triangular 'lateen' sails. These sails could be used even when the wind was not blowing in the right direction

Early steamships still carried sails

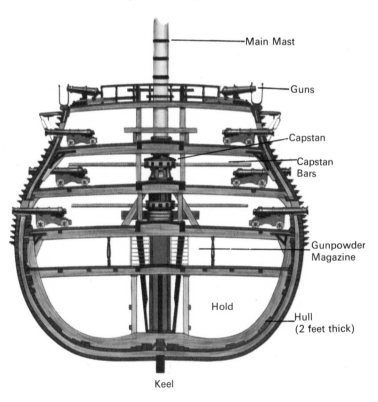

Diagram showing the inside of Admiral Nelson's ship the 'Victory'

Main Mast

Guns

Capstan

Capstan Bars

Gunpowder Magazine

Hold

Hull (2 feet thick)

Keel

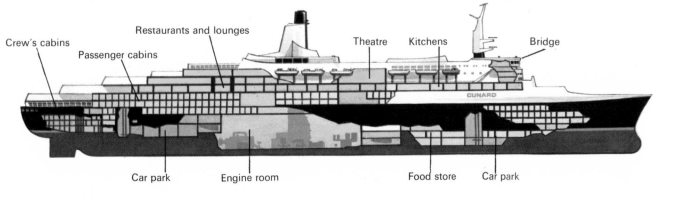

A diagram of the 'Queen Elizabeth II' showing the inside of a modern passenger liner

Crew's cabins

Passenger cabins

Restaurants and lounges

Theatre

Kitchens

Bridge

Car park

Engine room

Food store

Car park

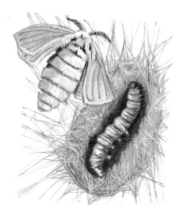

Silk moth and caterpillar in cocoon

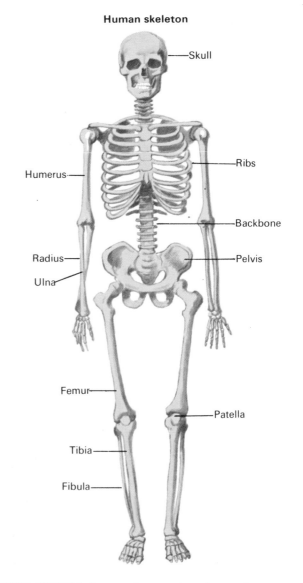

Human skeleton

Skull

Ribs

Humerus

Backbone

Radius

Pelvis

Ulna

Femur

Patella

Tibia

Fibula

The caterpillars will only eat mulberry leaves. They grow quickly. Soon they start to spin cocoons. They cover themselves with hundreds of yards of fine silk, stuck together with a kind of gum. The cocoons are put in warm water. The water washes away the gum. Then the ends of the silk threads can be wound on to reels. Now the silk can be dyed and woven into cloth.

For a long time only the Chinese knew how silk was made. They kept the secret carefully. Then, hundreds of years ago, two monks from Europe went to China. No one searched them when they left. But the walking sticks they carried were hollow. The monks had filled them with silkworms. Ever since then people have been producing silk in Europe.

SILVER For hundreds of years the metal silver has been used to make beautiful jewellery, plates and knives and forks. It is also used to make coins although most 'silver' coins do not contain much silver.

Silver is valued because it is soft and can be shaped easily. It also does not 'rust' easily. Sometimes it is used to 'plate' other metals.

Silverware

SKELETON A tent keeps its shape because it has a framework. Our bodies also have a framework. It is made of bones and it is called a skeleton. It is our skeletons that give our bodies their shape.

Our skeletons allow us to move about easily, because they are made up of many different bones. Where two bones touch each other there is a joint. The bones are shaped so that they can move easily against each other. They are held in place by stretchy fibres called ligaments.

SKYSCRAPERS In big cities many people live and work close together. Land is very expensive. So to save space on the ground men have learned to build very tall buildings.

Some of these buildings have about 100 storeys. They soar so high into the sky that they have been nicknamed skyscrapers. The first skyscrapers were built in the

United States of America nearly 100 years ago. They had iron frames. Now skyscrapers are made of modern materials like concrete and steel. They have to be very strong to stand up against the fierce winds that blow round them. Inside there are fast lifts to take people up and down. There are far too many stairs to climb to the top storeys.

The egg-eating snake can swallow a whole egg and then spit out the shell.

SNAKES The most feared of all animals are probably snakes but not many of them are dangerous to men. The largest group, which includes the grass snakes, is quite harmless.

Snakes swallow their food whole. Their jaws are not joined at the back so they can stretch apart like elastic. One good meal lasts a long time and the snake usually sleeps as it digests its prey.

Cobras and vipers can kill their victims with the venom which is released from the snakes' hollow fangs. One famous viper is the rattlesnake. Its tail ends in a series of horny rings which rub together and 'rattle' as it moves.

The boas and pythons are constrictors. They kill their prey by winding round the victim in a coil which gradually tightens and kills the animal.

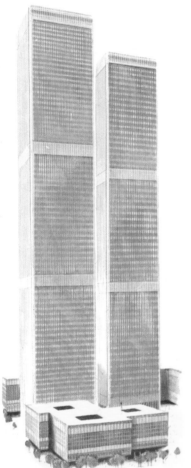

World Trade Centre in New York

SNAILS AND SLUGS Most molluscs are soft-bodied animals with hard shells. Snails have hard shells and live on land, in freshwater and in the sea. The water snails breathe through gills. The land snails breathe through lungs.

Slugs are also molluscs but they have no hard shells. They are pests in the garden because they eat the leaves of young plants.

Garden snail

Every snowflake has a different pattern

SNOW Clouds are made of millions of tiny drops of water. At the tops of the clouds the waterdrops are frozen into tiny pieces of ice. If they grow heavy enough they fall and bump into the other water drops which freeze onto them. As they pass through warmer air they may melt and fall as rain. But if it is cold enough they fall as snow.

If you look at a snowflake, you will see that it has its own beautiful pattern and that it always has six sides.

SOAP Try washing a greasy dish in pure water and see how long it takes to get clean. Add soap or detergent and the job will soon be done.

Soaps are made from animal fats or vegetable oils mixed with caustic soda or caustic potash. Caustic soda and caustic potash are *alkalis*. Detergents are made from the by-products of petroleum. Detergents clean things better than soaps, but they can be harmful. When waste containing detergents is emptied into rivers, the fish soon die.

Soap and detergents work in the same way. They wrap themselves round tiny particles of grease and dirt and float them away in the water.

SOIL If you turn over a spade of soil in the garden you will not see very much—just lumps of brown particles. But really the soil is teeming with life and goodness. Millions and millions of microscopic animals and plants live in the soil. Without them nothing could grow in the soil. When plants die, their remains, which are broken down by bacteria, forms 'humus'. The humus holds moisture and binds the soil particles into lumps.

Soil is formed from broken pieces of rock which roll down hillsides or are swept along by rivers, wind or ice. It is only when the remains of plants build up in the layer of broken rock particles that it becomes soil.

Listening to an engine through a metal rod

Engines are easily heard underwater

Sound travels through the air. It also travels through solids and liquids

SOUND When we hear sound, our eardrums are being made to *vibrate* (move to and fro) by sound waves in the air. The sound waves are a form of energy. We need two ears to tell us where a sound is coming from. Sounds in air travel more slowly than light. If you watch a man in the distance chopping wood you see the axe fall before you hear the sound of the blow.

We can tell sounds apart by their pitch, loudness, and quality. Pitch is the highness or lowness of a note. Loud sounds use more energy than soft sounds, and the vibrations of the sound waves are greater. The quality of sound differs because nearly all noises are made up of a mixture of sounds. If you shout in the middle of an open field the sound waves die away quickly, but if you shout in a large, empty hall, you hear a mixture of your shout and its echo off the walls.

Pictures of South America

Indians live in the Amazon jungles

Llamas live in the Andes

Mardi Gras

Gauchos herd cattle on the Pampas

Apollo spacecraft approaches the Moon

SOUTH AMERICA South America is the world's fourth largest continent (area of land). It has only about a quarter as many people as Europe, but it is $1\frac{1}{2}$ times as big. It is shaped rather like a pear. It is wide at the northern end, where the climate is generally very warm, and tapers down to Cape Horn in the south, where the climate is generally cold. It is linked to North America by a thin strip of land, the Isthmus of Panama.

A chain of mountains called the Andes runs from north to south down the western edge of South America. Many rivers run eastwards from the Andes. The biggest of these rivers is the mighty Amazon. A great deal of the northern part, either side of the Amazon, consists of hot, steaming forests full of snakes and wild animals. These animals include jaguars, sloths, armadillos, and giant anteaters. In the mountains are bears and llamas. In the southern part of the continent are wide plains, known as *pampas*. Many cattle graze there and crops are grown.

Before Europeans discovered South America nearly 500 years ago, American Indian tribes were the only people there. Some of them, such as the Incas, built big cities. Spaniards and Portuguese conquered the land, and their descendants still live there.

SPACE TRAVEL Travelling in space means going outside the Earth's *atmosphere*—that is, the layer of air and gases that surrounds the Earth and is really part of it. It is still a very new adventure. The first space craft, the Russian Sputnik I, orbited (circled) the Earth on October 4, 1957. And the first man to go into space was the Russian Yuri Gagarin, who made his space flight on April 12, 1961. The first man to land on the Moon was the American Neil Armstrong. He stepped from his spacecraft on to the Moon on July 20, 1969.

In order to travel in space, men have first to break away from the pull of the Earth, which we call *gravity*. It is this pull that makes a ball drop to the ground when you let go of it. To get away from Earth a spacecraft must be hurtled into the sky by a series of powerful rockets. Once it is high enough it can go into orbit—that is, circle round the Earth. Its speed keeps it from falling back to Earth, and gravity keeps it from flying off into space. In much the same way you can make a model aeroplane fly round and round you on the end of a piece of string. To go off into space, the rocket's engines must give a further thrust to break

Garden spider

Tarantula

Trapdoor spider

Black widow

away from gravity, just as your model plane would if the string were broken. When a spaceship nears the Moon, the Moon's gravity starts to pull it down to land. A big problem when a spacecraft returns to Earth is the Earth's atmosphere. The spacecraft rushes through the air very fast, and friction makes it hot. A special heatproof shield is needed to stop the spacecraft from burning up.

SPINNING AND WEAVING Most of our clothes and the fabrics we use in the home for curtains, blankets, sheets and upholstery are made by spinning and weaving fibres. Some of the fibres are natural, such as cotton and wool. Others are man-made, such as nylon.

Spinning means straightening out the fibres and twisting them together to make a long thread called yarn. The yarn is woven on a machine called a loom by passing one set of threads (the weft) under and over another set of threads (the warp). Alternate warp threads are raised and lowered and a shuttle carrying the weft thread shoots through the gap. The warp threads are then reversed and the shuttle shoots back again.

How a loom works.

Weft threads

Warp threads

Shuttle

SPIDERS There are about 2,000 different kinds of spiders. They all have eight legs and they can all make silk. Some of them use the silk to make webs to trap food. The garden spider's web is a delicate and complicated structure. When an insect is caught in it, the spider wraps it in silk and injects poison into it with its fangs.

Not all spiders build webs. Some like the wolf spiders run down their prey. The tarantula is a wolf spider. It is very big and it looks very fierce but its poison does not kill people. The only spider which is really dangerous is the black widow.

Trap-door spiders dig nests in the ground. Some have doors which fit like corks. Others have hinged doors and burrows with several tunnels so that the spider can escape from its enemies.

The crab spiders lie in wait in flowers. Their bodies match the colours of the petals and the insects that come for the nectar do not suspect that an enemy is lurking there.

The water spider builds its nest underwater. It carries bubbles of air on its body and preys on small water insects.

A sponge is a colony of tiny animals

SPONGE Many people use a sponge to wash themselves in the bath. The sponge they use is actually the skeleton of a colony of tiny animals. The animals are very simple. They live mostly in warm seas. The sponges attach themselves to rocks and draw in water through all the holes. The tiny animals that make up the sponge digest any little food particles in the water.

SQUIRREL The squirrel is a small furry rodent with a big, bushy tail. Most squirrels live in trees. Red and grey squirrels live in many parts of the world, although the red squirrel has been driven out of many places by the grey squirrel. Tree squirrels often build nests called dreys. In autumn they sometimes store nuts in hollow trees so that they have enough food to last them through the winter. They also eat insects, eggs and small birds.

Some of the squirrels live only on the ground. They are usually bigger and live on nuts, seeds and grass. They dig burrows in the ground.

A squirrel's nest is called a drey

STALACTITES AND STALAGMITES
Stalactites are stone columns which hang from the roof or walls of limestone caves, like icicles. They are formed very slowly when water trickles through the roof of the cave. When the water dries up it leaves a mineral called *calcite* at the bottom of the stalactite. If the water drips off the end of the stalactite, a stalagmite may build up from the ground, like an upside-down icicle. Sometimes stalactites and stalagmites join together like a pillar.

Stalactites and stalagmites

The first postage stamp was issued in England. It is called the 'penny black'. Today every country has its own stamps

STAMPS For many years people could send letters without paying for them! They were paid for by the people they were written to. But this system did not work very well. Just over a hundred years ago a new sort of post was invented in Britain. The people who sent the letters paid for them. And to prove that they had paid, they stuck a stamp on the envelope.

Now every country has its own stamps. They have all kinds of pictures on them. Many people collect stamps. They usually collect one special kind. Some people collect stamps with pictures of animals. Others collect stamps from one particular part of the world. Some stamps are worth a great deal of money. This is because there are only a very few of them in the world. This may be because only a few were ever made. Or it may be because just a few were printed with a mistake in the picture or the words. Many thousands of pounds have been paid for very rare stamps.

Perseus

Andromeda

Cepheus

Lion

Twins (Geminii)

Orion

STARS The stars we see twinkling in the night sky are like the Sun that shines during the day. But they look so much smaller because they are so very far away. Like the Sun, they are made of masses of gas.

Stars vary in size. Some are about the same size as our Sun, and some are smaller. But there are some giant stars which are hundreds of times bigger than the Sun. Stars are a very long way apart. If you think of our Sun as the size of a pinhead, then the next nearest star would be 10 miles away. Nobody knows how many stars there are. Astronomers, people who study stars, have counted thousands of millions of them, and there are probably many more.

The stars seem to move across the sky, and change their positions over several

The Crab nebula is a cloud of glowing gas. It is all that can be seen of a star which exploded hundreds of years ago. No star lasts for ever. Sooner or later each one will fade away and new stars will be born. The Sun, like every other star, will come to an end one day, but it will not be for a very, very long time

Right: Some of the constellations which ancient astronomers pictured in the sky. Many come from ancient legends

110

Hat spiral galaxy

Irregular galaxy

Elliptical galaxy

Spiral galaxy

Stars are grouped in huge clusters called galaxies. Galaxies have many different shapes. The Sun and its family of planets are in the spiral galaxy we call the Milky Way

months. But it is the Earth that moves, and not the stars. The movement that you see during one evening's watching is caused by the Earth spinning round like a top. The movement that takes place over several months is caused by the Earth rushing round the Sun. The stars also move through space, but we cannot see this movement because the Sun is moving with them.

Man uses the position of stars in the sky to help him find his way. One star, the Pole Star, is almost directly above the North Pole. If we can see the Pole Star, we can always find which direction north is.

Scientists believe that stars are born from clouds of dust and gas in space. A star begins to shine when nuclear reactions take place inside it. Atoms of a gas called hydrogen join together to make atoms of another gas called helium. Each time this happens heat and light are produced. Millions and millions of tons of hydrogen are changed to helium every second.

When all of the hydrogen gas has been changed to helium a star 'dies'. Sometimes it ends in a great explosion. Sometimes it glows red and then fades away. But stars 'live' for many, many millions of years.

SUBMARINE Submarines are boats built to travel underwater. They are usually shaped like a cigar, but more recent ones are fish-shaped. Submarines have a double body or *hull*, one inside the other. Between the two hulls are several tanks. When the submarine is going to dive, the tanks are filled with water to make the boat sink.

To make the submarine come to the surface again, the water is blown out of the tank by compressed air. Modern submarines are nuclear-powered and can stay under water for some months. Living is very cramped and uncomfortable in a submarine, and the sailors move about as little as possible to save their precious air supply from being used up.

SUGAR The sugar we use to sweeten our food is called sucrose by chemists. There are several other kinds of sugars, including glucose. Our bodies need glucose to produce energy. And we need sugar to make glucose. But many people eat more sugar than they need. The extra sugar is bad for their teeth and causes fatness.

All plants produce sugars but the sugar cane and sugar beet plants produce a lot. Sugar cane looks like bamboo and grows in hot, wet countries. The stems are shredded and squeezed in machines to get the juice which contains the raw sugar. Sugar beet grows in cooler countries. The roots of the sugar beet are sliced and boiled to get the sugar juice.

The sugar we use is made by refining, or purifying, the juice. The juice is heated and thickens to a syrup. Sugar crystals form in the syrup.

A submarine submerges by filling the tanks between its hulls with water. To come to the surface again the water is forced out of the tanks by compressed air

SUN Without the Sun, life on Earth would not exist. It provides us with heat and light, and enables plants to grow to provide food.

The Sun is a star, just like all the other stars you see in the night sky. But it looks bigger because it is very much nearer. If you travelled at the speed of light, you would reach the Sun in $8\frac{1}{2}$ minutes. But it would take you four years to reach the next nearest star.

The Sun is made up of a mass of hot gases, more than 100 times as big across as the Earth. Its surface is about 60 times as hot as a boiling kettle, and inside it is much hotter still. Sometimes dark areas, called *sunspots*, appear on the surface of the Sun. The planets, of which our Earth is one, spin round the Sun.

You must never look directly at the Sun. Its light is so bright it would blind you. People who study the Sun use special dark screens.

TAPIR A distant relation of the bad-tempered rhinoceros is the timid tapir. The tapir lives in the swamps and tropical forests of South and Central America and south-eastern Asia. It is about the same size and shape as a pig. It has short legs and a thick neck. At the end of its snout is a little trunk. It uses this trunk to hook food into its mouth. It feeds on water plants, twigs and fruit. Tapirs are fine swimmers.

TAXES Who pays policemen, or soldiers, or sailors, or nurses, and doctors? Who pays for our roads to be built, or our hospitals and prisons? In many countries the answer is 'we all do'. These essential people and things are paid for by everyone. This is done by taxes.

There are many kinds of taxes. For example, everyone has to give part of his wages—depending on how much he earns—to the government. This is called *income tax*. The richer you are, the more income tax you pay. The licences we need to use a radio, television, or car is another form of tax. Sometimes a tax is added to the price of goods we buy. This is an *indirect* tax. Such things as petrol and tobacco are taxed in this way. The person who decides what taxes we should pay and how much, is the Chancellor of the Exchequer. Each year he prepares a *budget*. It contains his tax proposals. He then asks Parliament to agree to these proposals.

Rates are another form of tax. They are paid by householders to the local council. The council uses the money for such things as schools, roads, libraries, street lighting, and welfare centres.

Tapir

Dark patches appear on the surface of the Sun from time to time. They are called sunspots

Great tongues of glowing gas leap millions of miles into space from the surface of the Sun

TEA One of the most popular drinks is tea. It is made from the leaves of the tea bush. Tea bushes are grown mainly in India, Ceylon and China. As the pickers move through the bushes they pick and sort the various kinds of leaves. Young leaves make the best tea. From the plantation the leaves go to a factory to be rolled and dried. Then the tea is packed in boxes and sent to all parts of the world. Much of it is sent to Britain which buys more tea than any other country.

When tea was first brought to western countries it was brewed in large quantities and stored in barrels like beer. Then the Chinese way of making fresh tea in a small tea-pot was used.

TEETH We use our teeth to cut, break up and chew our food. Many animals also use them to kill their prey. If you feel your teeth with your tongue you will notice that they are all different shapes. Some are sharp and pointed. Others are square and flat. This is because they are used for different purposes.

Animals such as lions and wolves that eat meat have long sharp teeth to rip the flesh. Grazing animals, such as cows and

Teeth of dog   Teeth of squirrel

giraffes, have rows of flat teeth that are used for grinding the plants they eat. Gnawing animals such as squirrels have two large front teeth. These can never wear away because they continue to grow all the time. Some snakes have special teeth—they are hollow and poison can be released through them.

TELEPHONE A telephone is an instrument that makes it possible to talk to someone who lives far away. The mouthpiece contains a microphone which changes sounds into electric current. The current flows along wires to the earpiece in the distant phone. The earpiece is a tiny loudspeaker which changes the current back into sound. Telephones are linked through an *exchange*. At the exchange an operator can connect your phone to the number you want, or

Picking tea. Almost three-quarters of the world's tea comes from India and Ceylon

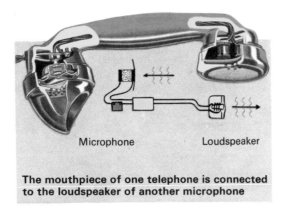

The mouthpiece of one telephone is connected to the loudspeaker of another microphone

you may be able to dial the number yourself and be connected automatically through the switching equipment. Radio telephones use radio waves to link the instruments. They are used to talk to people in ships, cars and aeroplanes.

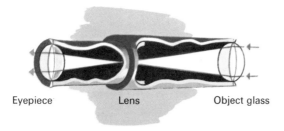

Eyepiece   Lens   Object glass

TELESCOPE A telescope is an instrument which makes distant objects look bigger. Telescopes are used for studying the Moon, stars and planets. *Refracting* telescopes, which are the simplest, have a lens called the *object glass* at one end of a tube, and a lens called the *eyepiece* at the other end. You look through the eyepiece, which magnifies the image formed by the object glass. You can focus the telescope to make the image clearer by making the distance between the two lenses larger or smaller. *Reflecting* telescopes have a mirror instead of an object glass to collect light from the object being studied. Reflecting telescopes can be used to see very faint objects.

TELEVISION Like radio, television works by turning the sound and the pictures into electrical waves that will travel through space. A television camera does not look at the whole scene in front of it like an ordinary camera. Instead, it looks at a little bit at a time. An electrical signal is produced that varies according to how bright or dull each area is. But the whole process is done so quickly that we appear to see a complete picture when we look at the TV screen. A colour TV camera separates the picture into areas of different colours as well as of different brightness.

TERMITES Like ants, termites live together in nests. They build their nests underground, in fallen trees or in great mud towers. The mud towers are sometimes three times the height of a man. Inside there are rooms, passages and storerooms like the inside of a great skyscraper.

At the centre of the nest is the 'royal chamber' where the queen lives with the king. The queen is very large and she does nothing but lay eggs. The workers look after the young termites and the soldiers guard the nest. They kill attackers with their great jaws.

Termites eat wood. They have been known to eat away the wood of a whole house.

THEATRE The name theatre comes from a Greek word meaning 'spectacle'. The earliest theatres we know of were in ancient Greece. They were open-air theatres. Rows of seats were built into a suitable hillside to form a large semi-circle. This was the *auditorium* and it might seat up to 2,000 spectators. At the bottom was the *orchestra*. This was a flat open space where the chorus sang and danced and the actors performed the plays. Behind was the *skene*. This was a building in which the actors changed their clothes and masks. The skene later developed into a stage. The word skene gives us the word scenery.

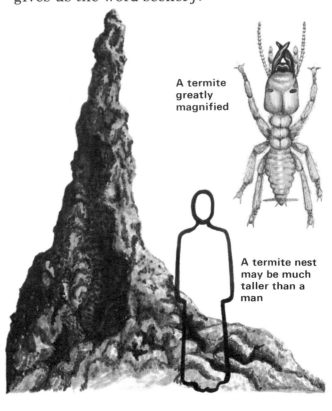

A termite greatly magnified

A termite nest may be much taller than a man

In Europe the earliest plays were usually acted stories from the Bible. They were at first performed in churches. Later, plays were put on in courtyards of inns or performed on carts in the streets.

The first real theatres were built in England at the time of Shakespeare. Shaksperian theatres like the 'Fortune' and 'Globe' were circular and they had no roof. They had a stage jutting out into the middle of the 'pit'. In the pit the 'groundlings' or poorer spectators stood. The wealthier sat in covered balconies. Actors wore the clothes of their own time. There was hardly any scenery.

Some years later, theatres similar to modern ones were built. They were completely enclosed. The stage was behind a 'picture frame'. The pit had seats. There was also movable scenery.

Some modern theatres have gone back to having a stage jutting into the pit. And many plays today need little or no scenery.

Most thermometers have mercury in the glass tube, but some have alcohol coloured red

THERMOMETER We use a thermometer to tell us how hot or cold things are. There are several different kinds, but the most common kind contains a white liquid metal called mercury. The mercury is put into a glass tube. When it is heated, the mercury expands, and travels up the tube. When it is cooled, it shrinks again. By marking a scale on the side of the tube, we can see what point the mercury has reached, and know how hot it is. The scale is marked in divisions called *degrees*. There are two kinds of scales in use, known as *Centigrade*, or *Celsius*, and *Fahrenheit*.

TIDES The waters of the great oceans rise and fall every day in movements we call tides. High tide is when the water comes right up the beach, and low tide is when the sea moves away uncovering wide stretches of sand. The tides are caused by the 'pull' of the Moon and the Sun. The Moon and Sun pull things towards them, just as the Earth pulls a ball towards it when you drop it. They can pull the waters of the sea about because water is flexible and moves easily. The Moon's pull has more effect on tides because the Moon is nearer the Earth than the Sun is. As the Moon goes round the Earth it pulls the tides up. So high tide is always on the side where the Moon is. It's also high tide on the other side of the world, because the Moon pulls the Earth slightly away from the ocean. There are roughly two high tides and two low tides every day.

TIGER Deep in the forests of Asia lives the biggest and fiercest member of the cat family—the tiger. The largest of the tigers are over twice as long as a man.

The tiger is a lone hunter. Its stripes help to hide it as it stalks through the forest looking for its prey. It hunts antelopes and wild cattle. Tigers will only attack a man if they are frightened or very hungry.

But man has attacked the tiger. In India the tiger has been hunted for its fine skin for hundreds of years. Now other countries have passed laws to stop tiger skins being sold, but it may still be too late to save the wild tiger. Very few are now left.

A tiger's stripes are good camouflage in the wild

Tornadoes can blow down trees and buildings

came from South and Central America. Today it is grown in many warm and dry parts of the world. The United States, Russia, China, India, and Rhodesia are leading tobacco-growing countries.

The tobacco leaves can be dried by leaving them in the sun. Another way is to dry or 'cure' them over a fire. After curing, the tobacco is stored for at least a year. It is then ready to be made into pipe, cigarette, or cigar tobacco, or into snuff.

TORNADO A tornado is a violent storm caused when the wind starts to whirl round and round in a small circle. It starts in a heavy black cloud. As it grows it drives a long column of cloud down towards the ground. If it reaches the ground the tornado can blow buildings and trees down, and carry people and cars for hundreds of feet. It moves on all the time, and its centre is never in one place for more than about half a minute. Most tornadoes occur in the central and eastern parts of the United States.

TORTOISES AND TURTLES No animal lives as long as the tortoise. In the Galapagos and Seychelles Islands there are giant tortoises that grow to a length of five feet and live for over 100 years.

Tortoises are slow, clumsy creatures that

TOBACCO People once believed that smoking tobacco was a cure for all kinds of illnesses. Doctors now know smoking is very bad for you. It is especially bad for the lungs.

Tobacco is made from the dried leaves of the tobacco plant. The tobacco plant first

Sea turtles come ashore to lay their eggs in the sand

feed on plants. When they are frightened, they can draw their heads and legs into their shells for protection.

Sea turtles are far quicker and fiercer than their relatives on land. Some are seven feet long and can swim fast with their powerful flippers. Turtles have to come on land to lay their eggs. This is hard work for the female. She drags herself up the beach, digs a hole, lays the eggs, covers them with sand and then struggles back to the sea. When the young turtles hatch they must find their own way to the water.

Many young turtles are eaten by birds and other animals. But the adults are hunted by man for their meat and their valuable 'tortoiseshell'. Their eggs too are collected for food and many kinds of turtles are now very rare as a result.

TREES Once most of Europe and North America were covered by great forests. Now the forests have been cut down to make way for farms, roads and towns. But trees are still very important and new forests have to be planted all the time to provide us with the wood, dyes, rubber, cork and many food crops, like fruit and nuts, that we need.

Most evergreen trees bear their seeds in cones and are called conifers. Among the most common conifers are the pines, spruces and firs. They grow mostly in the cooler countries of the world. The largest tree in the world is a conifer. The giant redwood of America often reaches a height of over 300 feet. Some of them have been growing for thousands of years.

Deciduous trees drop their leaves in the autumn and grow new leaves in the spring. Most of them have broad leaves and flowers, like the oak, ash, beech and maple.

UNDERGROUND RAILWAYS Thousands of people live and work in large cities. Thousands more visit the cities each day. And one of the greatest problems in cities is how to get all these people quickly and easily from one place to another.

Just over a hundred years ago the first underground railway was opened in London. It could carry people through tunnels beneath the streets. The trains were pulled by steam engines. They could not go

Oak

Palm

Beech

Redwood

Cycad

Pine

Cherry

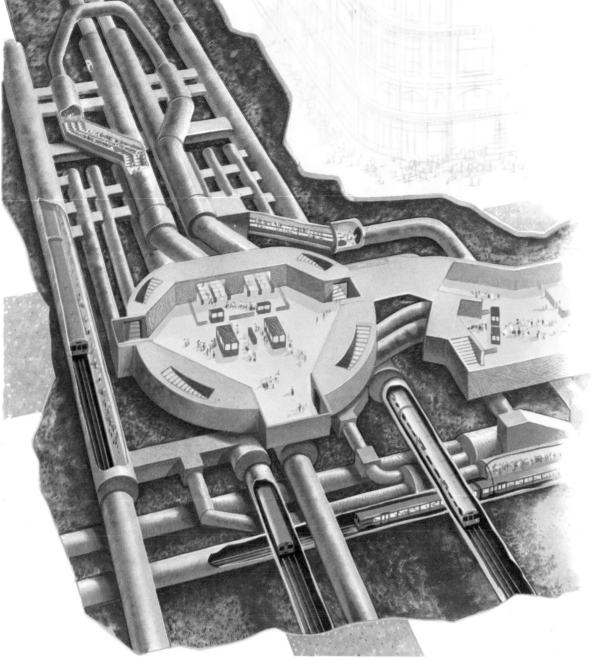

A large underground station is a honeycomb of tunnels leading from street level down to the trains and from one line to another. London's underground system was the first in the world and it is still the biggest. The New York City subway is also very large

far underground because there had to be openings to let out the smoke. And so they could not go underneath houses. But soon electric engines were invented. Now the trains could go deep underground. And they could go far under houses without disturbing them.

Today many of the world's largest cities are criss-crossed by a network of underground railways. Moving staircases called escalators often carry people down to the trains. Without these underground railways the traffic in big cities would be many times worse than it is now.

UNITED NATIONS In the lifetime of our grandparents two terrible wars have been fought. Because most of the world's leading nations took part, they were called World Wars. At the end of the Second World War the United Nations Organization was founded. The 50 nations who signed the Charter were, in the words of this Charter, 'determined to save succeeding generations from the scourge of war'.

Today the UN includes most countries of the world. The UN meets to settle quarrels between countries. It also tries to help remove some of the causes of wars—hunger, diseases, and lack of education. It tries to help poorer countries.

The Headquarters of the United Nations is in New York. Here the General Assembly and Security Council meet to discuss world problems.

They spend most of their time lying in herds along the Arctic coasts. They eat small sea creatures from the sea bed. In winter the walrus does not live under the ice and come up for air like other seals. It lives above the ice and defends itself from polar bears and other enemies with its frightening tusks.

Volcanoes are made of layers of lava and ash

A wasps' nest cut away to show the cells in which the queen lays her eggs

VOLCANOES

Most mountains are made of solid rock. But some mountains contain a pipe at the centre. The pipe goes deep down into the Earth's crust. At the bottom is red-hot liquid rock. It is called lava. Mountains like this are called volcanoes.

Sometimes the lava bursts up through the top of the volcano. This is called erupting. The lava carries with it bits of rock and ash and cinders. It flows down the side of the mountain. As it cools down it turns solid.

Some volcanoes erupt quite often. Others are quiet for many years. Some volcanoes have not erupted for hundreds of years. They are called extinct volcanoes.

WALRUS

The fiercest creature in the Artic is the walrus. Some walruses are over 10 feet long and weigh more than a ton. They are related to seals and have long, sharp tusks.

The walrus has sharp tusks

WASP

The yellow and black stripes of the wasp serve as a warning to animals and people that it has a nasty sting. The wasp is a hunter. It uses its sting to catch caterpillars and other small animals to feed to its young. Some wasps live in nests. They make the nest from 'paper'. They chew wood in their mouths and when it is soft they use it to make the paper cells in which the queen wasp lays her eggs.

Water vapour

Water

Ice

WATER

People and animals could not live without water to drink. Plants need it in order to grow. In fact, water forms about two-thirds of our bodies. Fortunately, water is one of the most common substances there is.

Water as we know it is a liquid. When it becomes very cold and freezes, it turns into a solid substance—ice. If we heat water until it boils, it turns into water vapour and disappears into the air. Water will even

Porpoise

Dolphin

turn into water vapour with the heat of the Sun. We call this process *evaporation*. If you leave a saucer of water out in strong sunshine for a few hours, it will all evaporate leaving the saucer dry. But the strangest thing about water is that it is formed from two gases, oxygen and hydrogen. When they are mixed together a spark will make them explode—and turn into water.

WATERFALLS Among the most exciting sights in the world is a huge waterfall. A great river pours over a cliff and falls hundreds of feet. The water thunders and splashes at the bottom. The sun makes rainbows through the clouds of spray.

Waterfalls come about when the ground over which a river is flowing changes from hard rock to soft rock. Over hundreds of years the water can only wear away a little hard rock. But it wears away soft rock very quickly. So the river makes a deep step down.

Some waterfalls are quite small. But others are enormous. The most famous are the Niagara Falls between Canada and the United States, and the Victoria Falls in Africa.

WEATHER When we are talking about what kind of day it is—warm, cold, wet or dry—we are talking about the weather. The weather is really the condition of the air around us, up to a height of about 10 miles above the Earth.

The heat of the Sun causes changes in the weather. Near the Equator, the Sun makes the air hot. Hot air rises, and cooler air from other parts of the world moves in to take its place. This causes wind. Masses of air, some of them hot and others cold, move about over the surface of the Earth. Some of them carry clouds with them, which bring rain. The weather stays fairly constant near the North and South Poles—where it is always cold—and near the Equator—where it is always hot. In between, in what we call the *temperate zones*, it can vary a great deal. But weather forecasters—men whose job it is to study weather conditions—can usually tell us what kind of a day we are likely to have.

WEEDS Some plants grow where they are not wanted. They are a nuisance in gardens and on farms. They are weeds.

Most weeds are hard to kill because they make new seeds quicker than other plants.

Blue whale

Some also grow from underground rhizomes which are very hard to remove completely. The worst weeds are those that strangle other plants. Most of them are parasites, like the dodder, which take their food from other plants and slowly kill them.

The speed of the wind is measured by an instrument called an anemometer. This has metal cups which are spun by the wind. The cups are linked to a dial which shows the speed of the wind

WHALES The largest animal that has ever lived is the blue whale. There are not many blue whales left now because whalers have hunted them for hundreds of years for their valuable blubber—the layer of fat beneath their skin—and for their meat.

The blue whale is a baleen whale. Baleen whales have no teeth. They have strips of 'whalebone' hanging in their mouths that act as a huge strainer. The whale gulps in water and, as it closes its mouth, the water

Whales have been hunted for many years and there are very few left of some kinds

flows out through the strainer and leaves the tiny planktonic animals and plants behind. This is the only food that these great creatures eat.

Toothed whales include the sperm whales, dolphins and porpoises. They have proper teeth and feed on all kinds of fish as well as squids and octopuses and even other whales.

Whales are warm-blooded animals and are the only mammals that never come on to the land. They can dive very deep in the water but they need to come to the surface for air. When they breathe out, you can see a great spout of steamy air coming from the whale's back.

WIND The air around us is very rarely still. We call moving air wind. Some wind is so slight we can hardly feel it. But the wind can blow so hard that it uproots trees and damages buildings. Wind is caused when hot air—heated by the Sun—rises. You can feel that hot air rises by holding your hand over something warm, such as a cup of tea. As this hot air rises, cold air from elsewhere moves in to take its place. Near the North and South Poles, the wind tends to blow from the east. Further away from the Poles, the wind tends to blow from the west. Towards the middle of the Earth, the wind tends to blow from the east and towards the Equator.

Wolves

WOLF Man has always tried to stamp out the wolf. It is a fierce animal related to the dogs. It has thick fur and large, powerful jaws. Once wolves lived in most parts of Asia, Europe and North America. Now their forest homes have been cut down and they only live in the far north.

The wolf has been hunted by man because it eats small animals and attacks sheep and other domestic animals. Wolves hunt by night in packs. There may be as many as 30 animals in a pack and their howls are a frightening sound.

WOOD The wood in a tree or shrub gives the stem support and helps to hold up the heavy branches. It also carries water from the roots to the leaves.

Each year a tree grows a new layer of wood. You can tell the age of a tree from the number of rings in the trunk

Most conifer trees are softwoods. The wood is used for making furniture and for making paper. Oak, poplar, mahogany and beech are hardwoods. Their wood is used for building and for furniture. Once all the ships in the British navy were built from oak because it is so strong.

So much wood has been used in the past that many forests have been destroyed.

WOOL Thousands of years ago men wore the skins of sheep to keep them warm. Then they learnt that they could clip off the sheep's woolly fleece without hurting the animal. They took the fleece and combed the tangled hairs until they were straight. They then twisted them together to make wool thread.

Wool is light to wear but it is very warm. It can be dyed any colour and it can easily be washed clean. Men have made many wonderful new materials for us to wear. But they have never been able to make anything better than wool.

WORMS The earthworms that live in the garden are useful animals. They break up the soil, letting in air, water and compost.

Not all worms are as useful. Some, like tapeworms and liverflukes, live as parasites in the bodies of other animals. Leeches suck the blood of other animals.

Many worms live in the sea. Some of them live in tubes in the sand and put out tentacles to catch their food.

Some worms are very wonderful. You can cut them into several pieces and each piece will grow into a new animal.

X-RAYS X-rays are invisible electrical waves, similar to those which carry light or radio signals through space. Photographs of the body taken with X-rays show up where your bones are, and help doctors to find out what is wrong with a sick person.

Yeast is used to make bread dough rise.

YEAST Yeast is a microscopic fungus which is only a single cell. It is very important to man because it is used to make beer and bread. When yeast is added to the baker's dough, the tiny plants feed on the sugar in it and release the gas carbon dioxide. This makes the dough 'rise'. Without yeast the bread would be hard and flat when cooked.

ZEBRA Unlike its cousins, the horse and donkey, the zebra is very difficult to train. Zebras are only found in Africa where they roam the grassy plains. The most noticeable thing about the zebra is its black-and white or brown-and-white stripes. These stripes, in fact, help to camouflage the animal. They break up its shape and blend with the background. Zebras stand about five feet high. They have quite short legs. But they can run swiftly when alarmed. There are three kinds of zebra. The rarest is the long-eared mountain zebra of southern Africa.

ZOOS There are thousands of different and exciting animals living in the world. It would be sad if we could see only the animals that live wild in our own country.

Zebra

But for hundreds of years men have been collecting animals from other countries. These collections are called zoos.

Animals in zoos are kept in cages to stop them from escaping. The cages are as large and comfortable as possible. Monkeys have trees in their cages so that they can climb about. Animals, such as polar bears and seals, which like to spend a lot of time in water have pools to swim in. Birds are kept in high cages where they have room to fly. Some animals are kept in specially warm rooms. In some zoos there is so much space that the animals do not have to be kept in cages. Instead they live in large fenced enclosures.

Zoos let us look at strange and interesting animals. They also help to save rare animals from becoming extinct. Many rare animals are bred in zoos.

Animals are looked after carefully in zoos

INDEX

125